ONE
Ancient & Modern
CHURCH

David S Hawthorn

Acknowledgements:

Cover image by David & Irene Bloor
with grateful thanks to the church of
St. Werburgh, Hanbury, Staffordshire

Many thanks to Jill, Gwen and Scott for their insightful,
constructive and helpful comments on the early drafts.

Thanks also to Alan Harris for proofreading the final text.

First published 2023

ISBN 978-1-9997082-3-8

A CIP catalogue record for this book is available from the British Library

Typeset, printed and bound in Poland.

Contents

Introduction

There is a well-worn joke that preachers tell, indeed I think I have used it maybe a dozen or so times myself. It goes like this; There once was a Christian sailor who was shipwrecked and castaway alone on a desert island. He endured years and years of his solitary existence through prayer, worship and calling to mind the passages of scripture he had memorised as a child, until one day his prayers were eventually answered and the column of smoke from his fire was spotted by a passing ship. On landing on his island, the captain of the rescue ship greeted the bearded survivor fascinated to learn how he had manged to live and eat for so long alone. The Christian explained about his faith in Jesus and how he knew his God would always sustain him. On showing the captain around the area that had been his home for so many years, the captain couldn't help but remark on the elegance of the three buildings that he had erected.

"What are they?" he enquired.

The castaway explained that the first one was his home, the second his church. The captain looked inside both and congratulated the Christian on their construction and decoration.

"But what about the third building?" the captain asked, "You haven't told me what that one is."

The Christian's face dropped and with a dismissive wave of his hand he said,

"That's just the church I used to go to."

As I said, it is well worn and you have probably heard it before, but the point is nonetheless very poignant. The humour, of course, is derived from the fact that Christians are so used to finding something wrong with the church, that even if they were the only one in attendance, they would still find some area of disagreement forcing them to move to a different one. It's funny because it is, in the main, an all too accurate observation. And for the sake of full disclosure, I too have left four churches; though in my defence, two of those were due to relocating across the country. But the point stands. Christians move church.

How Many Denominations Are There?

If we accept that we Christians, sadly, have a propensity to move church is it any wonder that, according to research carried out by The Centre for the Study of Global Christianity (CSGC)[1] in 2020, the 2.5 billion Christians worldwide attended 4.1 million individual congregations, and that those congregations belonged to 44,800 different denominations or rites.

That is a huge number of denominations. Before we go any further let's take a rigorous look at how they came up with that number. The CSGC defines a denomination as: 'An organized Christian church, tradition, religious group, community of people, aggregate of worship centre, usually within a specific country, whose component congregations and members are called by the same name in different areas, regarding themselves as an autonomous Christian church distinct from other churches and traditions.'[2]

The first thing to stress is that they do not count individual congregations as separate denominations even if they are completely distinct from all other congregations. There must be multiple congregations, have a central infrastructure and an agreed set of beliefs for it to qualify as a denomination. That sounds safe to me.

Secondly, they count similar denominations in different countries as being distinct. In some cases, I think this is probably defendable. For example, whilst both being constituent members of the Anglican Communion, we can consider the Church of England and the Anglican Church of Rwanda as separate entities with independent leadership and diverging opinions on some

---

[1] 'Status of Global Christianity, 2020' The Centre for the Study of Global Christianity at Gordon Conwell Theological Seminary.
[2] www.gordonconwell.edu/center-for-global-christianity/research/quick-facts/

matters of doctrine. The same can be said of the national members within the Lutheran World Federation, the Baptist World Alliance, the World Communion of Reformed Churches, the World Methodist Council, and others. However, considering the Catholic Church in each country as being a different denomination is probably less sound as they are all part of a single structure and there is broadly unified doctrinal adherence. The same is true, though to a lesser extent, within the major parts of the Orthodox Church. Removing all the Catholic and Orthodox duplication would probably reduce the total by no more than a thousand.

Finally, the CSGC include denominations that self-identify as Christian, but which are widely considered as not holding to the mainstream Christian faith (more on that definition later).

These details mean that I am not entirely comfortable with the 44,800 total as it stands. Whilst the exact number is probably incalculable, itself a sad indictment, I am going to arbitrarily half it and use 22,400 denominations in my ongoing discourse for no other reason as it feels more defendable than 44,800.

The Premise

Let that sink in. Not 22,400 different churches, but 22,400 different types of church; the vast majority of which lie within the protestant affiliation with its emphasis on personal interpretation of scripture, freedom of expression, and ever-unfolding present-day revelation. And yet, the Bible tells us very clearly there is just One Church. On the night before He was crucified, Jesus prayed,

'That they may be one even as We are one,'[1] and
'That they may be perfected in unity, so that the world may know that You sent Me.'[2]

---

[1] John 17 v 11
[2] John 17 vs 23

And whilst this prayer may be interpreted to only concern His small group of disciples, it is widely accepted that is still applies to the Church today.

The Apostle Paul using the analogy of the Church being the Body of Christ, emphasises in several of his letters that there is but <u>one</u> Body.[1]

It is undeniable scripturally that **there is just One Church regardless of what we may observe around us.**

On the one hand, there is One Church and yet on the other there are patently thousands of them. How can we solve this conundrum? How can all these denominations still be One Church? Basic maths tells us that $22,400 \neq 1$.

The ability to find a way to hold firm to these mutually exclusive truths at the same time is a skill that the Church has perfected. We have, over the centuries, expertly developed some sleight-of-hand methodologies that allow this glaring arithmetic miscalculation to be nullified.

It is my contention that these well-worn excuses are wrong. Let me be clear before we go on any further. This book is about the fact that there is indeed One Church in a real and practical way, and not 22,400 at all. It is my intention to convince you of this proposition.

But, of course, you may already believe that. Hallelujah if you do. The challenge for us then will be to convert such an inner conviction into demonstrable and reciprocated actions. Unless the world can see real tangible love across the Church, then how will we ever fulfil,

'All will know that you are My disciples, if you have love for one another.'

---

[1] 1 Corinthians 10 v 17; 12 vs 1 & 20; Ephesians 4 v 4; Colossians 3 v 15

If the world cannot see it, they won't believe it; and let's be honest, we have been pretty good at painting a very public picture of division for the last 1700 years. It is the baggage of those centuries that can often frame our approach to this thorny subject. So, my one request of you is that you park any preconceived ideas of the nature of church, and allow my premise to receive a fair hearing. If afterwards you don't agree then that is fine with me, and I thank you for your considered attention.

If, however, you do accept the truth that there really is but One Church, and that we must act as one, then there is a glorious opportunity for us as we take a significant step towards becoming the Bride of Christ that together with the Spirit shall say with one voice, *'Come.'*[1]

Why did I write this book?

When I embarked upon writing the novel Ancient & Modern: The Search, I committed myself to doing detailed research on the history of the Christian Church. Unsurprisingly, there was a lot of it. As I dug deeper and deeper, I would often come across little gems, many of which found their way into the story as anecdotes that demonstrated a wider set of beliefs prevalent at the time.

I wasn't sure what I had been expecting, but if I am honest, I had assumed I would see a progressive restoration of the Church from an ancient 'bad' place to a modern 'good' one in preparation for Christ's return. Let me share a personal example to demonstrate this.

I was under the sub-conscious illusion that the present-day restoration of the gifts of the Holy Spirit was in some way evidence of this progressive improvement of the Church, as such charisms had been unseen since the Apostolic age. During my

---

[1] Revelation 22 v 17

research I was genuinely shocked therefore to discover verifiable evidence, including newspaper reports, of miraculous healings across New England in the late eighteenth century. Plus, in 1706, Christian prophets were ministering openly on the streets of London to such an extent that they too made the headlines. Even further back I found that the well-respected church fathers Irenaeus, Tertullian and Cyprian, in a period spanning the end of the second and start of the third centuries, all defended the practice of speaking in tongues. Irenaeus wrote "We have many brethren in the churches having prophetical gifts, and by the Spirit, speaking in all kinds of languages." [1] My assumption that the gifts of the Holy Spirt was evidence that the Church was being progressively restored was entirely wrong. With my eyes opened I was then ready to learn whatever lessons history was going to teach me.

Repetition

Trawling through book after book as the research and writing continued over a period of four years, what I couldn't help but discover was that history really did repeat itself. I know, it is a clichéd phrase, and most people understand the principle, but I was genuinely surprised to see that in this church-centric microcosm of world history it appeared to be especially true.

The first thing that I saw was that there were successive waves of Christian awakening, or 'Moves of God' if you prefer. These tended to be centred around either a person (Luther, Wesley, etc.) or a place (Herrnhut, Azusa Street, etc.). These new Moves often encapsulated the rediscovery of a Biblical truth, never a new truth but the restoration of an ancient one that had, in some way, lapsed.

In most cases each Move led to the establishment of a new denomination, though that was rarely the original intent as most were borne out of a genuine desire to renew the existing

---

[1] Adversus Haereses, Page 6, Irenaeus (approx. 180 AD)

Church. Luther wanted to restore the Roman Church, not replace it. John Wesley, an ordained minister in the Church of England, resisted every attempt to break away until finally the Anglican Church refused to send ordained ministers for the new churches he had set up in North America, thus forcing him to ordain his own.

This happened over and over again, often the adherents of a new Move becoming distinct from those followers of the old. In one or two cases the opposite happened with a denomination becoming established as a reaction against the new Move, seeking rather to preserve the established norm against, 'dangerous new ideas.'

As I studied further, it became apparent to me that there were two common features in every historic move of God. Two things that in one guise or another were almost always present, and neither of which were particularly healthy.

1. A disdain for the previous Move of God

I found that the participants in each new Move would choose to set themselves apart from those that came before them and usually the one that came immediately prior to theirs. Let me give you an example. The Puritans were so focussed on establishing the 'Kingdom of God' that many of them left what they saw as a repressive England and sailed on the Mayflower to start a Christian colony in the New World. The Church they were reacting against had itself thrown off what they considered as the corrupt and self-seeking Roman Catholic Church barely one hundred years previously. The radical, risk-taking reformation of the early sixteenth century was now seen as the old way and something to be rejected. Move the clock forward a further hundred years from the Pilgrim Fathers, and we find that the land they helped establish was in the revivalist evangelical wave of The Great Awakening of Jonathan Edwards and others; the fuel of that great revival fire being a reaction against the Puritan establishment with its ties to the state.

This is a cycle of dishonour. The heroes of The Great Awakening dishonoured the Puritan heroes who had dishonoured the heroes of the English Reformation. Every Move of God appears to want to distance itself from whatever came before rather than building on the foundation that it had laid.

2. A belief that they were the final Move of God.

Hindsight makes it easy to look back on those who were convinced that they were living in the final throes of history and that Christ's return was imminent. But at the time this was a very real and very motivating doctrine that was common in nearly all great Moves of God. Don't misunderstand me, we should all be living as if Christ will return, that is good and proper. But what I saw was a corruption of this idea which I found somewhat troubling. The assumption appeared to be that because a certain Move of God had happened, Christ is now able to return. And that He had been waiting all along for it to arrive.

Let me share an example. Most British people are aware of a time in British history when we executed our monarch. King Charles I was beheaded on 30th Jan 1649 and this ushered in an eleven-year period when Britain was a republic. Fewer people are aware however that the motivation for the civil war that ended in regicide was religious, the pro-Catholic King Charles being seen as the enemy of the reformist Puritans. Even fewer people are aware however that during the republic many in the British parliament, the so called Fifth Monarchists, considered that King Charles was the Anti-Christ and that the glorious millennial reign of Christ had now begun. As I say, hindsight gives us a perspective that makes such beliefs seem ludicrous but nonetheless it was a widely held view at the time. The belief that a historic Move of God was the final one was, I believe, borne out of self-centred pride. The belief that God has been waiting for a specific Move is pure arrogance. It is also inextricably linked to Remnant Theology which I will cover in depth later.

Consider an alternative. What might happen if when the next wave of revival comes and those caught up in the holiness, the prayer, the charisma, those whose every hour is captivated by the Holy Spirt, if those very people didn't fall into the historical traps of Dishonour and Pride. What would happen if they chose to honour those who had gone before, recognising that today is built upon the foundations that were laid yesterday. And they have the humility to understand that they were just one part of Christ's body and not the culmination of centuries of Church history. Who knows what might be unlocked if in the midst of revival, His people truly demonstrated both honour and humility.

Why a Manifesto

I decided to subtitle this book 'A Manifesto for Unity' as, like a political manifesto, it is a collection of ideas and aims that together seek to achieve a cohesive outcome; that outcome being church unity. Just like a political manifesto it should therefore be weighed and debated before it gets your vote (or indeed does not!).
And I've called it just A Manifesto not The Manifesto. We all have a part to play, and others will correct and add to what I am saying here. I make no claim that my ideas are perfect, and will humbly accept correction where I am wrong.

Notes and Definitions

A little detail before we start and perhaps your chance to embrace your first challenge.

Firstly, there are footnotes. In the main these are references to the source material relating to the text, which in most cases will be a Bible reference. There is no primary material in the footnotes.

Secondly, all Biblical quotations are shown in *italics* and are taken from the New King James Version[1] except in certain

---

[1] Scripture taken from the New King James Version®. Copyright © 1982 by Thomas Nelson. Used by permission. All rights reserved.

cases where the alternative translation will be shown in the footnote.

Thirdly, I will be exploring some very controversial doctrinal issues. In so doing I will not share my personal views on what I consider to be the right position. I do, of course, have an opinion, but that is not the subject of this book. Rather, I will focus on why such issues have become problematic within the Church and hope to lay down some principles that may help us undo the damage sown over centuries.

Finally, in this book I will use certain key terms as convenient shorthand, which each deserve a definition:

Congregation, by which I mean a local, usually regular, gathering of Christian believers, under a specific local leadership. Whether they meet in a purpose-built religious building, a rented hall, or in someone's home (or for that matter online!) is irrelevant. For my purpose if they have a coherent local identity, I consider them to be one of the 4.1 million[1] such local units worldwide.

Denomination, which I will use as a catch-all term to include all 22,400 different types of congregations, regardless of whether they consider themselves to be denomination or not. To be considered a denomination it must have multiple congregations, some sort of central infrastructure or identity and an agreed set of beliefs.

The Eucharist, which I shall use as shorthand for the typically weekly sacramental meal of bread and wine that is celebrated in remembrance of Christ's atoning sacrifice. Dependent upon which denomination you are from, you may refer to it as either: The Eucharist, Communion, The Lord's Supper, The Breaking of Bread, The Holy Mass, The Holy Sacrament, The

---

[1] 'Status of Global Christianity, 2020' The Centre for the Study of Global Christianity at Gordon Conwell Theological Seminary.

Blessed Sacrament, The Remembrance Service, The Divine Liturgy, The Divine Mystery, The Divine Service, Holy Qurbana, Holy Qurobo, Prosphora or Keddase. I had to pick one word for simplicity, but all terms are equally valid.

Christian, which is a description of an individual who has placed their faith in Jesus and committed their lives to Him wholly. Christian is therefore a term which is exclusively used to describe an individual, so in this book I will use it liberally in that context. When it comes to using the term to describe a congregation or a denomination, then it gets more complicated. For now, permit me to not make any attempt to define that use of the term, as I will take time to explore this thorny issue a little later. This is not only deliberate, but also gets to the very heart of my message. Attempting to write-down a definitive statement of beliefs, or often church practice, has been the direct cause of church fragmentation ever since the early church councils of the fourth century. Consequently, I am going to tread very carefully in this area. To be clear, I am absolutely convinced that there is a most perfect definition of what a Christian is, and that God the Father is in no doubt as to whose *'names are written in The Lamb's Book of life.'*[1] But I do observe that countless times in history and, to be honest, still today, many have attempted to take on the divine responsibility of deciding who is 'in' and who is 'out'. It cannot be our job to make such a choice, which is an impossible task, *'for the Lord does not see as man sees; for man looks at the outward appearance, but the Lord looks at the heart.'*[2] Many will understandably struggle with this idea. I am not trying to be vague about fundamental Christian beliefs (which I will cover in detail later), I am simply suggesting that maybe we do not have the right to exclude those who don't conform to our personal definition of Christian. Besides, if we did, you can be sure that we probably don't conform to theirs!

---

[1] Revelation 21 v 27
[2] 1 Samuel 16 v 7

As It Was, And Shall Be

1. Life in Aaron's Beard

The first thing I want to do is to take you on a journey, a dream-journey into the future. Before I bombard you with Bible study, church history, statistics, and my personal observations which hopefully may offer some new insight or challenge, let's start at the end.

I want to look into the near future. A near-future where the principles I am going to outline in this book are already fully operational across every congregation within the One Church in a specific town. A town I have called Aaron's Beard.

Pour yourself a coffee, settle down in a comfy chair and come with me as we climb aboard our DeLorean and embark on a time-travelling journey to this prosperous provincial town far away from the big city.

As we drive past the sign that announces: 'You are now entering Aaron's Beard – Please Drive Carefully,' we remark,
    "I bet the locals call the place AB for short."
Our destination is the large Anglican church, St. Aidan's which is easy to find, its steeple standing proud like a rallying post for the town. Having parked and approaching the church on foot we can't help but notice the huge poster dominating the notice board: 'Whatever the need – we are here to help you.' A great sentiment we think. It is only as we pause to read the next line that we see the debt counselling, drug rehab. and marriage guidance on offer are run by The Holy Church of St. Bartholomew, a Catholic church, a few streets away.
Our host greets us, and we remark on how unusual it is to see the events at one church so prominently advertised by another.
"We aren't advertising <u>their</u> event," he explains. "This help is freely available to all who need it, and is provided at... let me think... five, no six, different church premises across the town. St. Barts are better at running them than the rest of us, although

16

some members of the other congregations are involved, if they want to."

The question this revelation then prompts centres around what appears to be a glaring confusion. If someone attending one of these events then wants to join a church, they wouldn't know which church they were joining.

"I don't understand what you mean," he says before explaining that anyone who makes a profession of faith or even just shows interest in finding out more is passed to St. Cuthbert's Baptist church. They co-ordinate home visits for those who want them, and run weekly new-starters sessions where they go over the basics of the faith.

"The Baptist faith?" we ask.

Again, he says that he doesn't understand what we mean. He then goes on to say that the most powerful thing that happens in the New Starters sessions is when they play the: 'Find Your Place' video. Our curiosity encourages him to explain that this video involves the six church leaders each giving a five-minute introduction to the main congregations, explaining what they are each like and want makes them special.

"What everyone remarks upon," he says, "is how moving it is that after extolling the virtues of a congregation and presenting a compelling case to join it, it is only when they realise that the leaders are each promoting a congregation other than their own, then the people really begin to see love in action. That is when people commit, not to the church, but to God."

We comment that we wouldn't be sure if our present-day church leaders would even know what makes another local church special, let alone want to encourage people to go there.

He then explains that each of the regular church services and midweek meetings are scheduled not to compete with each other.

"You could attend every service in AB, if you wanted to... but it would be exhausting - I don't recommend it!" he says before continuing, "Also, special events such as Christmas and Easter are completely unified programmes with a variety of opportunities for the townsfolk to interact with us in whichever way works for them: traditional or casual, families or youth, daytime or evening. Lots of variety."

When we asked if these were the main forms of evangelism, he was aghast and put us right, explaining that it was St. Aidan's that led much of the street-work, schools-work, and other forms of outreach. He did then clarify that it was only that St. Aidan's co-ordinated it, the people involved were drawn from across all six denominations in the town.

He then leads us to the side door of the grand church building. As we enter, we remark,

"You seem to get a lot of interaction from across the different denominations here," to which he points out that a lot of that emanates naturally from the One Body Groups.

Historically each congregation had run mid-week small groups in people's houses dotted across the town. On some nights people would travel to a house group run by their own congregation, when there was one on their doorstep run by a different congregation. Having made the decision to open up the small groups to everyone and rename them all as One Body Groups, the overall attendance has rocketed as has the ability for people to find their place in the overall mission of the Church as a whole.

When asked what is taught in the One Body Groups, he explains that they are an open mix of fellowship, prayer, worship and bible-study.

"It is up to the OBG leader to decide," he says.

"But don't they need to be given specific material to make sure they don't stray into... well, into heresy?"

He then points out that before appointing an OBG leader, we first have to be sure that this is what that person is called to do. Problems came in the past when loyal people were just asked to be small group leaders, but now we wait for those with passion and the gifting to surface and it works perfectly.

Walking along a corridor we pass a noticeboard peppered with clippings from the local newspaper, Facebook posts and pages from news websites. We pause to view them, and he points out, to our surprise, two articles stating the Church's position on a particular news-worthy topic, although each article is presenting the opposite opinion.

"We decided some time ago that if any part of the Church had a strongly held position, we would all support their right to hold it, even if other didn't agree with it. Consequently, it is not uncommon to read that two church-people hold opposing views. The media used to have a field day with this, but when they realised that we were all cool with this situation they soon gave up trying to make a story out of us. Once, they even invited opposing parties to participate in a radio phone-in, but when the church folks just complimented each other, refusing to criticise their opposite number, it clearly wasn't going to be the news story the media wanted. In fact, when people started commenting on how positively the Church handled differences, the media dropped us entirely."

We walk into a room labelled church office, but which is devoid of any desks, filing cabinets, photocopier, or any people. We take a seat at as he pours us a welcoming coffee.

"Have you moved the church office elsewhere," we ask politely.

"Yes, to Saint Dominicans with the rest," he says.

He then goes on to explain that when they realised that each of the six congregations employed an administrator, most part-time (only the evangelical church being full-time) they decided to co-locate them all in one large open-plan office at the Eastern Orthodox church. Now, they cover each other so that it is as if all six have full-time staff, even the one congregation whose administrator retired last year and who hasn't been replaced.

We ask how this works, financially, especially where there is now one congregation without an admin person in the room.

"Does that congregation pay for admin services from the others?" we ask. Not an unreasonable question, but sadly met initially by a blank expression before our host took the time to explain that none of the congregations now had their own money.

"What?" we couldn't help but retort.

He patiently explained that they made the decision several years ago to pool all of their resources into one bank account. All donations go into it and that is where all expenditure is paid. Utilities, repairs & maintenance, printing, visiting speakers, missions... everything (including, of course, all salaries). And that means all the ministers are paid from the same account.

"How can that work? Don't some get central stipends from their denominations?" we ask. He replies to say that even these are paid into the same fund.

"Where your money is, so your heart will be also," he remarks, and it is hard to disagree – clearly their heart is set on unity.

As I say, this is just a dream. But that doesn't mean it is unobtainable. As I now begin to delve deeper, hopefully, we will discover the principles that could make such a demonstrable expression of unity a reality.

2. What is the Church's Destiny

Fantasy is all well and good, but this is a book about reality, albeit a reality that we may need to accept by faith despite the overwhelming evidence to the contrary we see around us.

If we can pragmatically accept that the Church we see today does not demonstrate *the perfect bond of unity*[1], then perhaps understanding what the Church is going to become, especially in the end-time period, will give us a good indication of the necessary direction of travel from here to there. Then, with our eyes of faith, we may well see what the One Church is destined to become.

I know that there is an all-too-tempting desire to look back at the Church in the days of the Apostles; and to try and shoehorn our present-day expression of Church into that which we see in the book of Acts. Tempting yes; but this is only half the story, and it will be just as productive for us to first look at the future before we look in detail at the past. In the following couple of chapters we will take a good look at the early Church to discover what it was really like, and I will make a pragmatic assessment of where I perceive today's Church is in comparison and show that we are a long way from the New Testament Church.

But first, we need to look forward to what the Church <u>will become</u>. If we all truly understood the end game of the Church, then wouldn't it follow that we would all work on improving the bits that are lacking and delete the unnecessary bits? As Paul said,

"Forgetting those things which are behind and reaching forward to those things which are ahead, I press toward the goal for the prize of the upward call of God in Christ Jesus." [2]

---

[1] Colossians 3 v 14 (New American Standard Bible)
[2] Philippians 3 vs 13-14

I understand that talking about eschatological theology will open a whole new can of worms, but it is hard to talk about church unity without having a solid grounding on what the One Church will look like as we move towards the end-times. Whether you consider those days to be within reach or in the distant future, the same thing is true. God is preparing His One Church to be His Bride. Consequently, if our present-day choices are at odds with God's end-time strategy then surely it follows that <u>we</u> need to allow Him to change <u>us</u> as He clearly isn't going to change His plans.

But before we discover what the Church will look like as the Bride of Christ, firstly, we need to tread on our first doctrinal landmine.

<u>To Rapture or Not to Rapture That is the Question</u>

We're only into chapter two and already I've stumbled over a hotly debated and divisive topic, namely:

"Will the Church be around during the prophesised end-time tribulation?"

There are a few well defended positions on this subject, which I can simplify as "Yes", "No" and "Maybe." Unsurprisingly, I hold one of them, but as I stated in the introduction the purpose of this book is not for me to weigh-in on such debates but to, hopefully, consider how the divisions have affected the One Church. You can tell me if I succeed at the end (of this book that is – not the end of the world).

So, in trying to make sense of a chapter on the end-time Church, let's take a few careful steps. I am going to simply outline five key features of the end-times which are generally accepted.

<u>The Great Tribulation & Worship of The Beast</u>

22

One of the things that it is widely accepted will happen in the end-times is the Great Tribulation. I won't attempt to expand on what that involves at this point, suffice it to say that a great time of judgement is prophesied to happen as God brings an end to this Present Age and begins the Age to Come.

Most scholars also agree that the rise of the antichrist will include the establishment of a new one-world political order that is contiguous with a new religion with worship centred upon the antichrist, or as he is termed elsewhere, the beast. This global religious movement will envelop all people except those whose names are written in the Lamb's Book of Life, who will refuse to bow the knee at great personal cost.

'All who dwell on the earth will worship him, whose names have not been written in the Book of Life of the Lamb.'[1]

The Great Apostacy

Several passages in the New Testament make it clear that before the end many Christians will follow false beliefs in what is usually called the Great Apostacy.

'In later times some will fall away from the faith, paying attention to deceitful spirits and doctrines of demons,'[2] and,

'That day will not come unless the falling away comes first.'[3]

Whether this falling away is prior to the rise of the antichrist or directly part of his religion is one of those debated points. Also, I acknowledge that some believe that this apostasy has already been fulfilled in today's Church. What is generally accepted is that a feature of the falling away is Deception. This

---

[1] Revelation 13 v 8
[2] 1 Timothy 4 v 1
[3] 2 Thessalonians 2 v 3

means that millions of people will be duped into following someone whom they genuinely believe to be an *'Angel of light.'* [1]

Let us be under no misapprehension, this religious deception will be complete and utter. It will be completely and utterly wrong, but it will be completely and utterly convincing such that many <u>will</u> believe it.

'Then many false prophets will rise up and deceive many. And because lawlessness will abound, the love of many will grow cold.' [2]

'Then if anyone says to you, 'Look, here is the Christ!' or 'There!' do not believe it. For false christs and false prophets will rise and show great signs and wonders to deceive, if possible, even the elect.' [3]

Don't assume it will just be the weak-minded and impressionable who will be deceived. Any Christian without a strong relationship with the genuine Jesus Christ backed up with a good understanding of end-time prophesy is at risk of misreading the signs, and potentially being led astray.

<u>Persecution & The Great Harvest</u>

Alongside the apostasy we also read of a great end-time harvest. Those believers who are not deceived will stand up as faithful witnesses to God in those days. The sobering bit is that they,

'Will be handed over to be persecuted and put to death,' and *'Will be hated by all nations.'* [4]

Anyone studying end-time Biblical prophecy, cannot but help read the words 'persecution' and 'martyr' repeatedly. It

---

[1] 2 Corinthians 11 v 1
[2] Matthew 24 v 11-12
[3] Matthew 24 v 24
[4] Matthew 24 v 9

doesn't seem like much of a choice, does it? On the one hand join the false one-world religion or on the other suffer persecution and even martyrdom.

Let me give you some good news. This will also be a time of phenomenal harvest for the Church with probably hundreds of millions of people committing their lives to Jesus. This great end-time harvest is all part of God's plan. Jesus is preparing His Bride and we read that in those days, despite the persecution, Satan will be overcome,

'By the blood of the Lamb and by the word of their testimony, and they did not love their lives to the death.'[1]

Not loving your life to the death is a big deal. You have got to be one hundred percent clear on what you believe. All the more reason to look properly into end-time theology long before those days come upon us, *'As a thief in the night.'[2]*

Let's summarise:
- The Great Tribulation
- One World Religion centred on the antichrist
- The Great Apostasy
- Persecution
- The Great Harvest

How you lay these out chronologically is dependent upon your eschatology, and such a debate would be outside the scope of this book. However, we can clearly see themes of deception and persecution alongside church growth.

Two churches

If you accept that these five features are all present in the end-times playbook then, regardless of your personal

---

[1] Revelation 12 v 11
[2] 1 Thessalonians 5 v 2

interpretation, it is not too big a stretch to consider that at some point there will be two churches on earth:

1) A false state-backed religion, sadly including a significant proportion of former church members who have been deceived, and

2) A persecuted and yet thriving Church.

If this is so, then the second Church cannot exist in the form we see it today. It can only exist as an underground movement and will most likely have become structurally de-centralised. It could be a movement that is potentially made up of millions of interconnected but independent mini-congregations, almost identical to how the Church existed throughout its first three centuries, as we will see shortly.

A foreshadow of this two-church phenomenon happened in the late 1930s in Nazi Germany (as I discovered in researching the book Ancient & Modern: The Search). On the one hand there was the public, state-sponsored, politically controlled and ethically compromised Reichskirche, or State Church. Opposing it was the Bekennende Kirche, or as it is usually termed the Confessing Church. This loose affiliation had neither constitution, hierarchy nor leadership other than one or two vocal champions such as Dietrich Bonhoeffer and Martin Niemoller. What was amazing was that in the troubled times of pre-war Germany, all previous religious identities were shelved almost overnight. Affiliation to Lutheran, Baptist, Methodist, or anything else no longer mattered. What was important was which side of the two-church divide you were on. The official, centralised one or the so-called rebellious, de-centralised one.

The Inevitable Progression towards De-centralisation

Looking toward the Church's ultimate destiny, as a fragmented thriving underground entity, there must at some point be wholesale de-centralisation, the establishment of local accountability with relationship based inter-dependency between congregations. Again, this is exactly the church of the first three centuries as we shall see.

It would be quite a shock and major upheaval if the Church had to scramble to establish such a network sub-culture on the day that persecution began in earnest. Perhaps we should accept movement in that direction as necessary preparation. If so, this would essentially mean that over time dependency upon central (denominational) structures will reduce, and we may see break-away congregations (or groups of congregations) becoming more and more common. If we accept that this is part of our required preparedness, then it would imply that we shouldn't resist any opportunity for the Church to exist in smaller units.

How bizarre! Here I am writing a book about church unity and barely two chapters in and I am advocating yet more fragmentation. Stick with me, we have much to cover to fully understand that true unity is borne out of love and acceptance of differences, rather than uniting under one common confession.

If we can accept that there will be an inevitable progression towards the One Church meeting in smaller and smaller units, which will eventually need to exist as an underground network, then there is, I believe, one further outworking that we'll need to accept, one of identity.

<u>Blurring the Edges</u>

We saw that in 1930s Germany, for each congregation that chose to oppose the Nazi regime, the traditional labels that were used to define them ceased to matter. Overnight, they became part of the loose affiliation known as the Confessing Church. They didn't unscrew the Baptist, Lutheran or Methodist nameplates from the church door, but those names really served little to define who they were within the context of the day.

The differences were there, but didn't seem to matter. Hold on to that thought. What happened was a re-prioritisation of identity and I believe we will see this continue as we move towards the end-times.

The changes wrought upon the global Church as a result of the COVID-19 pandemic have proven to be very illuminating with regard to identity and denominational loyalty. In the conversations I have had with people from a wide spectrum of church traditions, the common theme has been that the Church will not revert into its former state. There was a widely held belief that God was at work establishing something new for His Church.

Whether that was accurate or not remains to be seen, but what was clear was that for many, as the enforced lockdown prevented them from gathering once a week in their usual building this gave them permission to engage with the One Church in a hybrid pick-n-mix way. Utilising the power of online they watched the teaching from one congregation, worshipped along with another and, when permissible post-lockdown, met with folks from yet another. Having benefited from this freedom of choice, now in the post-pandemic period such a non-traditional position appears to have become more acceptable to many. It appears that to some degree the idea of a Christian engaging with just one congregation has fundamentally changed. Perhaps this is an irrevocable change. Perhaps this is part of God's 'new' for His Church. What is clear is that in a practical sense the differences between congregations has for many become less relevant. To some the differences between congregations has become blurred at the edges.

If so, then maybe it is a positive step in the right direction. In essence this is allowing people to begin to experiment with engaging with the One Church as a single entity. More on this later.

I know that such a change in engagement may cause real consternation for congregations regarding infrastructure, personnel and resources but it may be a change that is required if we accept that the destiny of the One Church is to be de-centralised.

Speaking with One Voice

Finally in this view of the future of the One Church is the glorious truth that Jesus is returning for His Church, as a bridegroom coming for His Bride. We know that this Bride will be pure and spotless, and will speak with one voice. The closing verse of the book of Revelation tells us that:

'The Spirit and the Bride say "Come!"' [1]

Let that sink in. One Bride, one Church speaking with **One voice**!

Could the Church today speak with one voice on <u>any</u> subject? I seriously doubt it. And yet we read that in the end-days that self-same Church will say, "Come!" A heartfelt plea for God to come and restore all things, remove sin and establish His kingdom on earth.

But wait a minute, look again. If we flip it around, we could say that Jesus chooses not to return <u>until</u> His Bride says, "Come." Not that God is waiting for the Church, but that He is preparing his Church by moving us in that direction now.

If this is true, we see that in the end-times the antichrist isn't just left to run amok and create havoc with the Church. On the contrary, we see the Bride (Church) going through a process of purification, removing every blemish to become pure and spotless, to be unified, ready for His return.

The destiny of the Church is one of phenomenal growth, faith, power and victory and all this from within the midst of

---

[1] Revelation 22 v 17

persecution. It will most likely exist as an underground, decentralised entity that has let go of its primary denominational identifiers as they ceased to be relevant.

Perhaps it will take such persecution to allow us to let go of the paraphernalia of our traditions, theologies, rites, style of worship, even our individual identities... to be able to focus on the only thing that matters. A cry with one voice of,

"Even so, Maranatha, Come Lord Jesus."[1]

---

[1] Revelation 22 v 20

3. What Did the Early Church Look Like?

Having looked forward into our shared ecclesiastical destiny, we are now in a better position to glance backwards, over our shoulder, at the early Church and discover what church-life was really like during its formative season. For the first three hundred years of its existence, there truly was just One Church operating in the world. What is even more remarkable is that this One Church had a local presence in hundreds of cities and regions and yet possessed no central organisational structure. These weren't easy times. The Church had to deal with serious external threats, new doctrinal challenges, and relentless persecution. And yet, amidst all this, the Church thrived to such an extent that it grew at a phenomenal pace; the likes of which we will probably not see again before the end-time harvest.

To help us understand how the Church operated during its infancy there are several sources to which we can turn; the most important being the New Testament which we shall use as our datum in the next chapter. But first, we are going to hear from the early Church fathers. These authors spanned the first two centuries of Church history, some knew the Apostles personally and learned from them; others knew those who knew the Apostles. They all held positions of leadership in this thriving new One Church.

I suspect that some people may baulk at the idea of referring to non-Biblical (or non-canonical) writings, and to be honest I was one of them for much of my Christian life. If that is you, let me ask you a simple question.

"Who wrote the four New Testament Gospels?"

That's it. It isn't a trick question. Can you name the authors of the first four books in the New Testament?

I assume most of you will have said Matthew, Mark, Luke and John. If you did, you are probably correct. Probably? How dare I say probably. I say probably because the authorship is not attested to in the gospels themselves. If you don't believe me, take a look. How do we know who wrote them? We are reliant upon the writings of Irenaeus, Eusebius of Caesarea and others to tell us who wrote those gospels. Likewise, if we ever say that Peter was crucified upside down, or that he was one of the first leaders of the Church in Rome, once again this information comes to us from contemporary extra-Biblical sources.

Also, before you dismiss these ancient texts may I ask if you have ever found modern-day Christian writers useful. One look at your bookshelf should answer that. Maybe you've gone further back and read Christian writers such as C.S. Lewis, G.K. Chesterton or John Bunyan. Even today you will find inspirational Christian quotes from Martin Luther, John Calvin, Thomas Aquinas and Saint Augustine readily circulating on social media every day. That being the case, what makes older writings any less valuable? Surely there is merit in reading the views of those who, in several cases, personally knew the Apostles, were appointed by them, whose teaching is largely the passing of the baton from the Apostles. Isn't it fair to say that older should, to some extent, be better?

Maybe so, but they aren't in the cannon of scripture for a reason. They are not gospel truth. Some of these old writings may be of dubious authenticity, and so we must tread carefully and lean upon scholarly consensus. If many scholars agree it is genuine, then it probably is. Thankfully, this is the case with the authorship of the gospels and the last days of Peter.

Much of the writings of the early Church fathers are doctrinal expositions; Bible commentaries; treatises against the heresies of the day; or defences of the Christian gospel. Amongst them however are some texts that simply describe aspects of church structure, practice and rite. These are known in scholarly circles as 'Church Orders.' In reading these we can gain a valuable insight into what church was like in the period immediately after the Apostles. By extension we may reasonably conclude, with some degree of confidence, that this was probably the way that the Apostles meant it to be.

The first Church Order we can consult is the oldest verified text of its time. It is entitled, 'The Lord's Teaching Through the Twelve Apostles to the Nations', but is more widely known by the Greek word for teaching: Didache. It dates from around AD150 and whilst its authorship is unknown, we know it was copied and circulated extensively and is quoted in many other later documents. It has two halves, one embracing some elements of doctrine, the other, simply a description of what church was like.

The second key document was written around fifty years later by Hippolytus and is known as the Apostolic Tradition. It is believed this was written by someone eager to preserve the Church as it was from specific heresies he felt were seeping into the Church. This too was copied, translated, widely circulated and quoted in later texts.

If this subject interests you, you may want to consider reading these texts. Both are widely available free of charge online, there being no copyright laws in the second century. In addition, during my research I have imbibed the writings of several other early church fathers including Clement of Rome, Irenaeus, Ignatius of Antioch, Justin Martyr, Tertullian, Origen, Clement of Alexandria, Cyprian and others as well as the extensive writings of the later church historian Eusebius of Caesarea.

What I am now going to present is my personal distillation of what I believe church looked like in its first three-hundred years, i.e. before AD312 when it became the religion of the then Roman Emperor. I will not provide specific references as I am not seeking to defend an argument but to stimulate thought. I do encourage you to make your own investigations. But this is my personal portrayal formulated from the above sources which are rightly open to interpretation by better scholars than myself. That being said - here goes.

Church Meetings

Meeting as a church was technically illegal in the Roman Empire and consequently meetings would typically be small and secretive, often in the homes of the wealthier members. Few would know the whereabouts of the church meeting, including many within the church itself. Whilst we don't know the numbers that would have gathered in one place, we can assume that it would most likely be in the tens, rather than in the hundreds. This would mean that in a city or across a rural area there would be dozens of small house-sized congregations that met separately but maintained the unified identity of the city or region church that they considered themselves to be part of.

Joining the church

It wasn't easy to join the church. Not only due to the secretiveness but more importantly because joining was not taken lightly due to the likelihood of martyrdom. Anyone making a profession of faith was asked to undergo up to three-years of rigorous instruction and 'testing'. During this time, they were not only educated in the scriptures, but their lifestyle was observed to see if they 'cared for the poor and widows' and that they 'led a moral and upright life'. Those in an immoral relationship therefore had three years to either get married or separate. Those employed in jobs incompatible with their faith would be expected to leave. This could mean that in addition to those working in the idol-trade and prostitution, sometimes it included soldiers. If, after three years they were deemed to be exhibiting the fruit of the Spirit, then and only then would they be baptised.

Baptism

Baptisms happened once a year, usually at the Feast of Passover. Converts would fast prior to their baptism date (as did much of the Church) which is the origin of today's Lenten fast. The baptism would ideally be by immersion in a river or stream, but if that wasn't available (bearing in mind they would need to baptise many converts, and often in secret) then they may use a pond, or the warm waters of the public Roman baths. Or, if all else failed, by pouring water over the head three times. All were equally acceptable. Once baptised they would be anointed with oil by the bishop and then, and only then, be allowed to call themselves a Christian. After their baptism they would be invited to participate in their first Eucharist, at which they would be given, in addition to the bread and wine, two extra glasses: one a glass of water, symbolising their purity: the other, a glass of milk and honey, signifying their arrival into the promised land.

Church Services

When the house-congregations gathered, the services would be more Jewish in style than you might have expected. They celebrated the annual feasts of Passover, Pentecost and Tabernacles. They kept the sabbath, although the regular meeting day would be on a Sunday not the Jewish Saturday Shabbat. When they did meet, they would almost always celebrate The Eucharist. Some of the members would then take the sanctified elements home in order to repeat the sacred meal every day until next Sunday. Also, the meetings would be more charismatic than most are today with the free use of the gift of the Holy Spirit. Healings, singing in tongues and prophetic words were to be expected.

Prayer and Fasting

Members fasted twice a week, on Wednesdays and Fridays and were encouraged to pray seven times a day. These regular prayer times would usually begin with reciting the Lord's Prayer either audibly if they were at home or silently if they were outside.

Church Governance

Each church (or collection of house-congregations) was under the leadership of a team of Presbyters. This word is often translated elder and is the word from which priest is derived. There could be a large number of Presbyters, as many as 86 in one city is quoted. There would also be a smaller number of Deacons assisting in practical matters. All congregations in a city or region were overseen by an Episkopos who ensured they did not stray from the truth.

Teaching

The teaching in each church (or collection of house-congregations) was overseen by one individual. The Bible uses the word Episkopos for this person, which is often translated as Bishop. He (they were exclusively male) was responsible for faithfully passing-on the teaching that he had learned from his Episkopos, and would use the Hebrew scriptures (our Old Testament) to explain the way of salvation and how Christ came to fulfil ancient prophecy. Bishops were elected from within their own congregation but were only appointed by the laying-on-of-hands by a group of neighbouring bishops. Bishops were entirely independent and of equal status to each other. There were no archbishops, or central structure of any kind. Whilst the bishops of five specific churches (Jerusalem, Antioch, Constantinople, Alexandria and Rome) did assume a higher status, this came later. Those bishops who were able to write, would do so, some extensively. Their writing would be distributed not only within their own church but might also be offered to neighbouring bishops. This was also the case with letters from the Apostles and other texts including the gospels. In time, many of these letters became common texts shared by all the churches in a region, some of the most impactful being re-read every week during the Sunday services.

Heresy

People relied upon their bishop to faithfully keep to the teaching passed-down from the former bishop and so-on back, just a few generations, to the Apostles. The main guardians against error were twofold: The Hebrew Scriptures (our Old Testament) in this pre-New Testament era; and mainly tradition. By tradition we simply mean the faithful passing-on of that which had previously been taught. False teaching, however, did surface and if a bishop was thought to be straying into error, he would expect to see an intervention. This would not come from his archbishop or patriarch as no such positions existed, but from his neighbouring bishops with whom a personal relationship had been fostered. If the wayward perpetrator refused to change, the final sanction was when his peers agreed that, for the sake of the truth, he must be officially excluded, or excommunicated.

Itinerant Ministers

In addition to the overseeing bishop and local elders there would have been occasional visits from traveling prophets and missionaries (or apostles) who would be permitted to stay for no more than two days. Interestingly, if these travellers ever asked for money for themselves, they would immediately be thrown out as false prophets. Apostles had no direct authority over specific churches, even those they had established.

Persecution

Throughout the first two centuries, gathering together for Christian worship in the Roman empire was technically illegal. The degree to which this was enforced was typically a local decision. This meant that every Christian lived under the expectation that a local reactionary persecution could flare up at any time. Fierce and bloody crackdowns might be enacted at seemingly a moment's notice. Consequently, the Church existed as an underground organisation. Sometime literally! There was therefore little scope for street evangelism or mass rallies. The gospel was spread mainly in two ways. Firstly, by personal word of mouth. Despite the risks, Christians were all too ready to jeopardise their personal freedom to share the faith in their hearts. The second way was public, very public. In a society where life was cheap and death was a form of public entertainment, the execution of Christians was commonplace. However, people saw that their martyrdom was unlike that of a common criminal or of a gladiator. "These people die, not for a cause, but for a person," they would say, with thousands converting as a direct consequence. No surprise that Tertullian later famously wrote, "The blood of the martyrs is the seed of the Church." All of those who died for their faith were honoured. Each year on the anniversary of their martyrdom (their so-called eternal birthday) their friends and loved ones would gather, not in their usual place of worship but in the underground catacombs where the remains of their fellow-believer were entombed. They would cover their tomb with a white cloth and share the Eucharist together, remembering the sacrifice of their friend, in the context of Jesus' final sacrifice for mankind. In time, the sheer number of martyrs meant that the days spent worshipping in the tombs would outnumber those spent elsewhere.

Phenomenal Growth

Despite the lack of any visible presence, the lack of any central hierarchy, the lack of a New Testament, and despite frequent and bloody persecution, the Church grew rapidly. According to some modern scholars its numbers swelled at a rate of 40% per decade,[1] rising to become a tenth of the entire population by AD313 when the Edict of Milan made Christianity fully legal. The scholarly consensus is that by this date, the Church in the Roman empire would have numbered around two million people.[2] This is a useful figure as we also know that when the first ecumenical council was held in AD325 at Nicaea all 1800 bishops from across the Roman Empire were invited.[3] This means that if the One Church across the empire had two million members and 1800 bishops, distilling these two simple figures shows that on average, a bishop would have been responsible for a church of

---

[1] "The Rise of Christianity", pp. 7-10. Rodney Stark, 1996
[2] "How Many Christians Were There in the Roman Empire?" Kyle Orton, 11 June 2021
[3] "What Was the Council of Nicaea?" by Ryan Nelson, Sep 14 2018. overviewbible.com

around 1100 people, itself a tenth of the population of a city or region. There was, of course, an equally great growth in the church beyond the Roman Empire but figures from Arabia, India, North Africa, Russia and beyond are not as readily available to us.

Overall

If we were to compare the early Church from this chapter to that which is postulated might be the destiny of the Church described in the previous chapter, there is much similarity; the most obvious being that there is persecution. But putting that to one side, we see: decentralisation; single identity; strong local presence; the importance of relationships; and the consequential phenomenal growth. They are all there.

Perhaps we shouldn't be so surprised about this. God designed his Church to be His Bride, and that is precisely what it will become. The problem is the spots and wrinkles we have acquired over the last 1700 years.

So, let's look at that very first Church and see how far from it we have drifted.

4. A Comparison with the New Testament Church

In the previous chapter I presented how I believe the early Church looked based on the writings of those who were within it. We saw that it was both a united body and also a collection of separate independent entities. Unity was not something that came from the dictate of a top-down hierarchy but more through the commonality exhibited between its overseeing bishops in close relationship with each other. This was a unity between peers in some way similar to the movement of a shoal of fish or the murmuration of starlings, which appear to act as one but are nonetheless made up of thousands of individuals in complete harmony with each other.

But I accept that my description did not come from scripture. So, let's look at the Church we see described in detail in the New Testament. The most important passage that can help us understand how church really worked, appears at the end of Acts chapter two. Here, we see plainly what happened in the immediate aftermath of the birth of the Church. Let's take a look.

'And they continued steadfastly in the apostles' doctrine and fellowship, in the breaking of bread, and in prayers. Then fear came upon every soul, and many wonders and signs were done through the apostles. Now all who believed were together, and had all things in common, and sold their possessions and goods, and divided them among all, as anyone had need. So, continuing daily with one accord in the temple, and breaking bread from house to house, they ate their food with gladness and simplicity of heart, praising God and having favour with all the people. And the Lord added to the church daily those who were being saved.'[1]

We have already seen how much importance was put on passing on the teaching of the Apostles, well this is the Church in

---

[1] Acts 2 vs 42-47

Jerusalem as fashioned by all eleven of the original disciples. This is their blank canvas. This was Church version 1.0 and as such must lay for us an essential foundation of what church is meant to look like.

There is a lot in this short passage and, if time permitted, we could spend a long time studying it, as countless better scholars than I already have. For my part I would like us to use this passage in the way it is presented, as a list – or a checklist. Simplistically, when I look at this passage, I see that Church 1.0 exhibited a list of traits. I make it <u>fourteen</u> in total.

These traits are all listed here in scripture for a reason, so we can be sure they must be important. We don't get a list about the Corinthian church nor the one in Rome, just this one – right at the beginning. So, I think it merits us to look through each trait in turn, doing two things as we go. Firstly, we will try to understand what they probably meant <u>at the time</u> rather than through the prism of today's religious viewpoint. Secondly, I will try to compare this checklist with the church I see today, which inevitably will be from a western viewpoint. I will try to assess whether these traits are present or absent from the modern church. In so doing we should get a sense of how far we've drifted from the original template. To keep it simple (and for my own amusement) I'm going to give each a score out of 5 stars, then take an average at the end. Feel free to make your own evaluation if you want to. Here goes.

1. The Apostles doctrine.
    During the first century, any reference to 'scripture' would only refer to the Hebrew scriptures (i.e. the Old Testament), which were used liberally to explain the way of salvation opened by Jesus as a fulfilment of prophesy. But things were very new, and the people would be hungry to understand more. The Apostles, having had three years emersed with Jesus plus the baptism of the Holy Spirit, had the answers the people needed. By Acts chapter 2 none of this was written down, so it was a case of everyone listening, accepting, and allowing their faith to build. It is here that the principle of 'passing on' the Apostles teaching began, a principle we see evidenced across the early Church.

Eventually this teaching was written down in what we now have as the New Testament.

Where are we today? In most denominations, both the Old and New Testaments take centre stage. To what degree the teaching is adopted is open to debate but scripture is nonetheless widely visible across the modern Church so I will give a 5-star rating on this one.

2. Fellowship

From the Greek word koinonia, which means 'holding something in common,' fellowship is more than a time of shared tea and biscuits. It holds the idea of mutual and open cooperation in both worship and God's work. As an organisation whose whole premise is based on love, if we were to consider fellowship within a particular congregation then we could probably score it highly. But, considering honestly the depth of self-sacrifice and cooperation between denominations, we would have to admit that it was, at best, sporadic. There are even parts that refuse to worship together. Overall, that's just a score of 2 out of 5.

3. Breaking of Bread

Some might interpret this phrase as simply eating together but I believe it is a clear reference to the celebration of the Eucharist. Almost every congregation is committed to the importance of this act. But notice that Breaking of Bread does appear twice in the passage, the second one raising the idea that the Eucharist was performed both daily and from house to house. We've already seen that this was indeed the case in the early Church. The reverence and honour with which The Eucharist is upheld across most denominations would mean we could score it highly, but the fact that we have boxed it into a weekly (or sometimes monthly) ceremony, held in a sanctified place means I'll have to wind it back to just a 3 out of 5.

4. Prayer

Just like the Eucharist, prayer is part of the fabric of most church services. Whether it be liturgical or spontaneous it is nonetheless a core part of Christian worship. Notice how, at the beginning of the passage. we see that these first four attributes: Teaching, Fellowship, Breaking of Bread and Prayer were things they *continued steadfastly.* We have seen that members of the early Church prayed at least seven times a day every day. We need to look beyond the weekly service to identify if we are really 'continuing' in prayer. But prayer is a personal thing. To help me decide I went looking for hard facts and found the 2014 Religious Landscape Study carried out by the Pew Research Centre.[1] One of the questions asked concerned the frequency of prayer and of the 24,000 Christians surveyed, those who prayed at least daily ranged from 54% to 80% dependent upon denomination. A figure that was higher than I'd thought and pushes the score up to 4 out of 5.

5. A sense of Awe

I fear this term has become somewhat neutered over the centuries. To get a better idea of what was originally meant by 'Awe' we need to look into the Hebrew. The word translated 'Awe' is *yirah* which can mean respect or reverence but is most commonly translated as fear or awe. The root word itself is strongly connected to trembling. The English word Awe, itself originates from the early Scandinavian words for terror or dread. Today many, but by no means all, denominations engender a strong sense of reverence. Few would expect to witness a sense of trembling in the presence of an almighty God. Some would consider that something might be wrong with those so affected. Consequently, I should really give a nil score on this one, but perhaps temper it to a half, in recognition of the holy reverence of some denominations.

6. Signs & Wonders

It would have been easy to lump this aspect with the previous Sense of Awe. But to do so would be to dilute the Awe (or Fear) due to God's majesty and power, turning it into no more than wonderment towards His acts. Miraculous signs and wonders were evident throughout the Book of Acts, and have continued to be attested to in extra-Biblical writings of the time and throughout the history of the Church, even up to the present day. But is it fair to consider this as a core part of the everyday life of every denomination? Probably not. Consequently, the lack of the common-place, every-day miraculous (unless that is an oxymoron?) only permits a score of a half out of 5.

---

[1] https://www.pewforum.org/religious-landscape-study/frequency-of-prayer/

7. Being Together

All who believed were together. We have already looked at the principle of Fellowship, or common purpose. The Greek phrase used here is the same as earlier in the chapter when they were all, *'in one place'*[1] or a few verses prior as *'a gathering'*[2] and a couple of chapters later as *'gather together.'*[3] Clearly, the early Church saw a priority to physically meeting together. Returning to the 2014 Religious Landscapes Survey, 17% of those who call themselves Christian stated they would attend a religious service 'Seldom' or 'Never'. The situation in Britain is much worse. According to the British Social Attitudes survey 2014 the proportion of those who call themselves Christian and yet never attend a religious service was a whopping 54%.[4] Looking on the bright side a large number of believers do still regularly attend (US 45%, UK 30%) so overall I can give us a 3 out of 5.

8. Had all things in common

This suggests that the early Church could be described as communist, or at least some form of community. Whilst devoid of the more recent Marxist, Leninist, Trotskyist connotations, it is nonetheless clear that there was not only a belief in common ownership, but that it was actively practised. It is difficult to suggest otherwise, particularly when you add in Jesus' teaching that *"whoever of you does not forsake all that he has cannot be My disciple"*[5] This is probably the most contentious part of this checklist and worthy of much deeper debate than we can allow without getting bogged down. My constraint was just to present what it probably meant to that Church in Jerusalem, and it clearly appears that they *"had all things in common."* Next time someone suggests becoming a New Testament church, perhaps we should point this out first! Today, outside of monastic orders and a handful of non-mainstream communes I'll have to score this a resounding zero.

9. Divided them among all, as anyone had need

---

[1] Acts 2 v 1
[2] Acts 1 v 15
[3] Acts 4 v 26
[4] British Social Attitudes Surveys (1984) extracted from faithsurvey.co.uk/uk-christianity.html
[5] Luke 14 v 33

The Church in Jerusalem embraced re-distributing wealth according to need. Isn't it amazing that whilst common ownership is almost completely absent from the modern church, the heart attitude to help those in need is nonetheless living and very active. The Christian Church is known to do more than just 'collect for the poor' as most world religions do. It has an in-built good-works ethos that is driven from a deep-seated love for humanity and desire to respond to visible needs. As Augustine put it *"Charity is a virtue which, when our affections are perfectly ordered, unites us to God, for by it we love him."*[1] As we shall see in a later chapter there is even a plethora of Christian ministries that exist solely to meet the needs of the poor and disadvantaged. I am pleased to give a 4 out of 5 on this one, after all it is something that we're known for.

10. Daily with one accord in the temple

This is an important and oft misunderstood one. On face value it may appear to suggest that they attended church every day, but I don't believe that is the point being made here. Besides, we already covered their frequent gatherings earlier. The first congregation was exclusively made up of Jews from across the Roman Empire.[2] They had a clear understanding that Jesus was their Messiah, and their conversion was not to a new religion but to the Messiah who fulfilled their scriptures.[3] It follows therefore that they would spend time with other Jews sharing the wonderful message of salvation. Therefore, I believe that this is less a comment on attendance, more about recognising that Jesus was the fulfilment of Hebrew prophecy and the quest to convince the Jews of the day to recognise their Messiah. Understanding that Christianity is born out of, and ultimately reliant upon, its Hebrew roots[4] is an important truth that has largely been lost to the Christian Church. As we will see in a later chapter this deception began with the heresy of Marcion of Sinope in the early second century and led to the very first fracturing of the One Church. As to the present day understanding of the relationship between the Church and Israel, I will have to give just a half out of five, again.

---

[1] Quote of Augustine of Hippo widely attributed. Extracted here from www.britannica.com/topic/charity-Christian-concept
[2] Acts 2 vs 9–11, 41
[3] Matthew 5:17
[4] See Acts chapter 11

11. Ate their food with gladness and simplicity of heart

(NB I already covered the house-to-house element earlier).

Sharing a meal together is a powerful act of togetherness and it would appear that in the early Church they knew how to enjoy their food. The phrase 'gladness and singleness of heart' comes from the Greek word *apheloteti* which means generous. We can assume that these shared mealtimes were joyful affairs where generous portions of food and drink were shared between friends. In short, they were unashamedly feasting and thanking God for each other. Sharing meals together does vary from culture to culture, and whilst I would like to think that those within the Church participate more than those outside, I've no way of knowing. I think a 3 out of 5 is as neutral as I could go.

12. Praising God

In the midst of the feasting, the meeting of needs, the awe, the signs & wonders, the togetherness, the sacraments – they praised God, the source of all. Whilst praising God is more than just singing, worship is as much a core part of church services as prayer and The Eucharist. Anecdotal evidence would suggest that a large proportion of the Church doesn't attempt to limit worship to just within their services, but rather encourages it to pervade everyone's lifestyle. A hearty 4 out of 5 is probably justified.

13. Having favour with all the people

We need to note that by Acts 2, no persecution had yet been enacted against the fledgling Church. And yet the reaction of those outside of the Church was unqualifiedly favourable. What about today? What do people think of Christians? My quest for evidence led me to a survey carried out in 2015 by Com-Res,[1] one of the questions asked to non-Christians was to describe a Christian they knew. The top answers were Friendly and Caring (both over 50% of respondents) followed by Good-Humoured, Generous, Encouraging and Hopeful (between 20% and 40%). I must admit, that was quite a surprise. The negative terms (Narrow-minded, Hypocritical and Boring) barely registering on 10% of respondents. Much to my surprise I think I can score this 4 out of 5.

---

[1] Taken from talkingjesus.org/wp-content/uploads/2018/04/Talking-Jesus-dig-deeper.pdf

14. The Lord added to the church daily

It was exclusively the Lord who added souls to His Church, and he did so every day. This is interesting as in the previous thirteen points, other than *'sharing with one accord in the temple,'* we saw no missions, evangelistic campaigns, street-work, door-to-door, seeker-friendly services or Alpha courses. This kinda turns the textbooks on church growth on their head, doesn't it! Are people being added every day today? According to the 2015 report by Christian Trend Watcher,[1] the global Church is growing at a rate of 1.18% p.a. which, if you permit me to play with the numbers, works out at a global average of just 7 people per congregation per year. Hardly adding day by day. Sorry but that is only a 1 out 5 but at least there is some growth.

So, where does that leave us. Firstly, I will have to finish this audit by collating these individual scores with all fourteen attributes all equally weighted. We find that today's Church scores just 2.5 on The Acts Two scale:

I'm not sure what I had expected so let's just reflect on why I've just done this arbitrary exercise.

We had a look at the early Church, the one that grew phenomenally over the first three centuries and which was based on the template cast in Jerusalem after the day of Pentecost. If today's Church is not only disunited but also is no longer growing at the pace it was in the first centuries, then perhaps looking at that original template is valid.

It would appear that our arbitrary scale suggests the Church has drifted 50% from its original manifestation. What would be interesting would be to do the same scoring exercise upon the Church at key moments in its history. Say, in AD325 (the time of the Council of Nicaea); in 1045 (at the time of the Great

---

[1] Taken from www.christiantrendwatcher.com/blog/the-status-of-global-christianity-in-2021

Schism) and immediately pre- and post- the Protestant Reformation of 1517. But I will leave this to more academic experts than myself to do that.

So, we have glanced over our shoulder, back-in-time, <u>and</u> we have looked ahead at the Church's end-time destiny. What is clear is that the Church we have today, in all of its 22,400 different iterations, looks like <u>neither</u> of them. We are not where we started, and we are not where we need to end up. The question is therefore,

"Are we honest enough to acknowledge where the Church is now and open enough to allow God to fashion us into the One Church that He destined us to be?"

This is the quest of this book. If you are not convinced, then park the book here. If you are ready to embrace change then read on. We began this book with a glimpse at a fantasy. The reality may look much different, but the essential choice is do we stay as we are or are we willing to become the One Church He designed.

To help us moving forward I have identified four specific challenges ahead of us.

Challenge 1: How can we shake off structures that have been acquired over the last centuries that maintain a habit of fragmentation?

Challenge 2: How do we deal with the real and sometimes polarising differences between us?

Challenge 3: What does it mean to act with real unity such that those outside of the Church would notice? and,

Challenge 4: How could the One Church really function in practice.

I have structured the rest of this book to look at each of these challenges one at a time.

Challenge 1: Dismantling the Structures of Division

5. The Get Out of Jail Free Cards

We, the Christian Church have become unconsciously adept at sidestepping the need for visible unity. Don't get me wrong, we are brilliant at uniting with those congregations and denominations whose expressions of church-life and doctrinal emphasis are broadly like our own, but there are subconscious limits. Although we do tend to be polite and civil towards those congregations and denominations with whom we may fundamentally disagree.

This, I believe, is achieved because we have developed a number of subtle excuses that allow us to exercise such tolerance. These pervasive, damaging, and entirely unwritten and unspoken beliefs have become entrenched across the Church when it comes to the subject of unity.

These excuses are what I like to term the 'Get Out of Jail Free' cards that we unknowingly keep up our figurative vestment sleeves ready for the moment when we are forced to confront face-to-face the One Church vs many denominations numerical mismatch.

Hopefully you don't hold any of them, let's see.

Card 1 – The Bible is Wrong

First of all, there is the option that the Bible is wrong and the implication of there being just One Church is a mistake. Being of the school of thought that the Bible is infallible I cannot accept this so I will have to discard this excuse straightaway. If you, dear reader, do not accept the infallibility of scripture I suggest you pass your copy of this book to someone who does, as it probably isn't going to help you at all. I am going to be using a lot of scripture alongside learning points I have discovered from church history to build my argument.

Card 2 – Church Doesn't Matter

Secondly, is the view that Church as an institution doesn't matter and to a large extent can be ignored. Let me expand. We know that to become a Christian one has to make a personal commitment to Jesus. It is a specifically and wholly personal decision which Jesus responds to, and the Holy Spirit enters and fills our lives. Or at least that is my simple explanation. Church as an institution is not part of that personal commitment despite the commitment often being made during an event that is linked to a specific congregation or denomination. Consequently, it is possible to acquire the unstated belief that commitment to a specific congregation and attending their services is entirely optional. Holding to this belief allows any interaction with other Christians to be unencumbered by the denominational affiliation they may have, as each individual is treated as... well, as an individual, rather than a Methodist, a Baptist, a Charismatic or a Catholic.

This is not an entirely bad attitude and one in which there is some merit. However, to believe that church affiliation is optional is a misnomer as we automatically become part of His Body from the moment of salvation.

'So we, being many, are one body in Christ, and individually members of one another.'[1]

There is a specific God-ordained purpose for that. We are meant to support each other, suffer with each other and rejoice with each other.

'But God composed the body... that there should be no schism in the body, but that the members should have the same care for one another. And if one member suffers, all the members

---

[1] Romans 12 v 5

51

suffer with it; or if one member is honoured, all the members rejoice with it.' [1]

Love for God, being the first commandment, is immediately followed by love for each other. The Christian life is one of relationship.

'Jesus said to him, "You shall love the Lord your God with all your heart, with all your soul, and with all your mind." This is the first and great commandment. And the second is like it: "You shall love your neighbour as yourself."' [2]

And not only that, but God has also designed structure into His Church, a structure which includes leaders and teachers who are there to help us.

'Remember those who rule over you, who have spoken the word of God to you, whose faith follow, considering the outcome of their conduct.' [3]

I suspect that some of those with a casual attitude to congregational affiliation may be those who have been hurt by previous church experiences and now exist in a pseudo self-protection mode.

Card 3 – Other Churches are Dead or Wrong or Both

The third Get out of Jail Free card is the widely held yet rarely articulated view that the vast majority of churches are sadly lost in their own traditions, dead religion or error. This belief implies that God has been steadily shrinking His Church over the centuries in order to create a perfect, refined and pure bride.

Cutting through the super-spiritual language, it is the belief that one part of the Church is 'right' and the rest are, not to

---

[1] 1 Corinthians 12 vs 24 - 26
[2] Matthew 22 vs 37 - 39
[3] Hebrews 13 v 7

put too fine a point on it 'wrong.' This is largely the basis of what is known as Remnant Theology which I will cover in detail in a couple of chapters. I can see that such a belief would be rather tempting if you've backed the winning team, but please consider one very important caveat. Those who hold to this teaching (as unstated as it is) are exclusively members of the denomination which is the purified and true part of the Church. I am yet to hear anyone suggest that their own denomination is not part of the near perfect remnant! Also, it is interesting to note that despite this belief being strongly held, it is rarely articulated as such. It is almost as though it would be embarrassing to admit it, especially with other denominations listening. Which of course it is - not just embarrassing but entirely shameful.

If it were to be true that God, in purifying His Church now has one favoured denomination, then by implication it must mean that there are 22,399 denominations that are impure, out of favour and to some extent wrong. I wouldn't want to be the person having to let the members of all the wrong denominations, some 2.5 billion people, know that despite their years of faithful service, personal devotion and self-sacrifice they didn't quite make the grade. Of course, I am being a little extreme, but this is the logical extrapolation of the belief that a large proportion of God's Church is dead.

Bear in mind though that salvation is exclusively a matter for the individual. Consequently, a proportion of every denomination, of every congregation may well be unsaved and as such are not part of the One Church regardless of the faithfulness of their attendance. In joining a congregation, we are not joining a social club or a self-help group. It is not meant to be our hobby. Personal faith in Jesus immediately thrusts us into His global family called The Church and without that faith we have nothing. Our relationship with The Church is therefore a consequence of our personal relationship with God, not the other way around. Therefore, we mustn't substitute faith in God for faith in our local congregation, or denomination or indeed the One Church.

We will take a closer look at how the Bible says we should relate to other denominations and congregations a little later.

Card 4 – The Church Universal vs The Church Local

The fourth and final Get out of Jail Free card, or theory as to how 22,400 denominations can actually be just One Church, is perhaps the most widely held. It hinges on the idea that there are two ways of thinking about church. It is often articulated as follows:

"There is the Church <u>Universal</u> and the Church <u>Local</u>."

The Church Universal being a spiritual entity that encompasses every congregation and denomination worldwide, whereas the Church Local being its representation on a congregation-by-congregation basis within a specific geography. Again, this is a tempting philosophy, principally as it allows us to shamelessly employ a double-minded attitude to our inter-church relations. On the one hand I can say with all sincerity that I am in complete unity with another congregation or denomination; whilst simultaneously refusing to actively do anything with them as I don't agree with their liturgy, doctrine, hierarchy, style, people, or one of countless other reasons. As long as unity can be marginalised into an ethereal spiritual dimension then we don't have to do anything about it, it doesn't affect us, and we can distance ourselves with a clear conscience from whomever we disagree with. Surely this cannot be what God desires for His Church?

When Jesus said, *'By this all will know that you are My disciples, if you have love for one another.'*[1] I don't believe He followed it with 'Terms and Conditions Apply.'

He didn't state that we were to have love for those with whom we agree, or those who share our interpretation of

---

[1] John 13 v 35

scripture, or those who sing the same songs, or pray the same prayers, or dress the same. No, the <u>commandment</u> He gave us was specifically to *'Love one another as I have loved you '[1]* and how did Jesus demonstrate His love for us? It wasn't theoretically, He didn't love us on a technicality so that He didn't have to get personally involved. No, God demonstrated His love for every one of us in a real and tangible way, despite us rejecting Him at the time.

'God demonstrates His own love toward us, in that while we were still sinners, Christ died for us. '[2]

God <u>demonstrated</u> His love for us, while we were against Him. We are <u>commanded</u> to love each other in the same way. This, of course, applies not only to our fellow believers but we are also commanded to show love to everyone, even our enemies[3]. However, when we consider other Christians, we learn that we are *'individually members of one another'[4]* which takes it to a substantially deeper level.

In other words, **our love for other Christians must be demonstrable not just theoretical, regardless of whether we agree with them or not**.

If you are able to accept this principle, then you are ready to take this journey with me. But first, pop those Get Out of Jail Free cards back into the deck, put the lid on the box, and put it away. Remember you are going to need an open mind as we move forward.

---

[1] John 13 v 34
[2] Romans 5 v 8
[3] Matthew 5 v 44
[4] Romans 12 v 5

6. Why Ecumenism is Destined to Fail

According to the Encyclopaedia Britannica, Ecumenism is a "movement or tendency toward worldwide Christian unity or cooperation."[1] To entitle this chapter as I have does raise the understandable reaction, "But surely you are pro-ecumenism?" You would have thought that given the subject matter of this book I would be one of ecumenism's principal banner-wavers. Sadly not, so it is incumbent upon me to explain why not.

Before I do let me make a clear distinction between two very different inter-denominational activities that often share the Ecumenical name. On one hand there is a growing drive to build relationships between congregations and denominations, which is to be applauded. This is entirely around relationship building and to some extent shared activity. Many of those involved in this work are called Ecumenical officers or such like. I have no issue with this; in fact it is to be actively encouraged.

This chapter however is entirely focussed on the movement whose express aim is to unify all denominations into a common confession, rite and Eucharistic worship. This quest for church uniformity has been an active pursuit for over 1700 years; it is not a new concept and is still being pursued today.

'The ultimate goal of ecumenism is the recognition of sacramental validity, eucharistic sharing, and the reaching of full communion between different Christian denominations.' [2]

Or, as the World Council of Churches (WCC) defines its mission as facilitating, *'the way to visible unity in one faith and one*

---

[1] https://www.britannica.com/topic/ecumenism
[2] "Toward Full Communion" and "Concordat of Agreement": Lutheran-Episcopal Dialogue, Series III. William A Norgren & William G Rusch, Wipf and Stock Publishers.

eucharistic fellowship, expressed in worship and in common life in Christ.' [1]

This Ecumenism seeks to remove the differences between denominations and as such, I believe, is destined to fail. Not due to the lack of prayerful effort by those involved in the detail nor from lip-service from the respective denominational leaders. It is a goal that cannot be achieved as the goal of Ecumenism is unity through agreement, or if I may use a more provocative word, unity through uniformity. Agreeing what the church believes. There is a great temptation to bring the leaders of major church denominations (or at least their representatives) together to agree a 'common confession.' This sounds particularly attractive when it comes to trying to reach agreement on any thorny issue. And this is not a recent strategy but has routinely been the practice for the last two millennia.

Historical Failures

History has shown that the convening of an Ecumenical assembly to debate and hopefully agree a common position has usually resulted in a position being reached which some party(s) cannot accept. Consequently, they cannot agree to it and must declare themselves to be separate. This would appear to be the exact opposite of the convocation's original intention, although sadly many were staged politically to achieve that specific goal.

Let's take a look at some of the more notable points of fracture within the Church that came about as a result of bringing the churches together into an Ecumenical gathering.

324 The Council of Nicaea. A common statement of beliefs was agreed which had the effect of ending of Jewish practices within the Church and forcing the separation of the **Messianic Church**. We'll study the Nicene Creed in detail in a later chapter.

---

1 https://www.oikoumene.org/

451 The Council of Chalcedon. Called to agree a definition of how Christ's divine and human natures interrelate (or don't). Its outcome was the separation of the **Oriental Orthodox** and **Coptic churches**.

867 – 870 The Councils of Constantinople. The topics debated were mainly church governance, and the role of icons and images in worship. Decisions forced through led to the eventual separation of the **Eastern Orthodox Church** in 1054.

1529 The Marburg Colloquy. The leaders of the German and Swiss reformations met to agree on several doctrines. However, disagreement on transubstantiation meant they couldn't unite, separating the **Lutheran Church**.

1618 The Synod of Dort. The doctrine of **Arminianism** was opposed by a strongly **Calvinist** (pro-Predestination) council, the outcome being a major fracture in the Protestant church.

1643 The Westminster Assembly. This was convened to agree which form of church governance was to prevail in post-Reformation England. The resultant Act of Uniformity gave rise to many separatist movements including the **Puritans** and **Baptists**.

And yet to the present day we seek to repeat this mistake and continue to dialogue in the full knowledge of the harm it will do not only from within the Church but also to the Church's reputation outside.

The Modern Ecumenical Movement

There has been a lot of Ecumenical activity over the last eighty years. I will attempt to give a brief overview and I apologise in advance but there will be quite a few acronyms.

The key event happened a little after 10:00 in the morning on 23rd August 1948 when, in the Amsterdam Concert Hall, representatives of 147 churches passed a resolution that brought the World Council of Churches (WCC) into being. An ironic name, as despite its aspirations its very title emphasises the plurality of its membership. As its first general secretary Willem Visser't Hooft later said, "The word 'churches' in the name indicates our weakness and our shame before God, for there can be and there is finally only one Church of Christ."[1]

This movement didn't start in 1948, the appetite for cross denominational dialogue had been building since the start of the century with various bodies and national ecumenical movements convening, but 1948 was when it got serious. Today the WCC includes within its membership all of the major denominations with the notable exception of the full participation of the Catholic Church.

The WCC does much good work in providing aid for refugees, but its most important and extensive activity is in its Faith and Order Commission. This body seeks, through dialogue amongst its 120 members, to agree a common confession in the areas of Faith (matters of belief) and Order (matters of structure and governance).

Several Protestant denominations are, for several reasons, opposed to the work of the WCC so have formed themselves into their own collective, which eventually became the World Evangelical Alliance (WEA). In an ironic twist in 2015 the WEA announced plans for closer cooperation with both the WCC and the Catholic Church's Pontifical Council for Promoting Christian Unity (PCPCU).

---

[1] #WCC70 Amsterdam 1948 (2): Covenanting in work: What on earth is the World Council of Churches? Extracted from www.oikoumene.org

Since the 1960s proactive restorative discussions have been set up by the PCPCU which have made important steps to reconnect with both the Eastern Orthodox and the Lutheran churches. A significant step towards normalising relations between the Orthodox and Catholic communions was taken by the Second Vatican Council in 1965 when both parties lifted their mutual excommunications of each other, some 911 years after they were enacted. Despite the growing dialogue and compromises made by each side, the sticking point is the subject of authority, the very cause of the original schism. Back in 1054 the reason for the Catholic/Orthodox split was ostensibly because the Catholic Church had unilateral inserted a phrase into the Nicene Creed. This, however, was merely the final straw that exposed the self-imposed supremacy of the Roman church. Most consider that any attempt to unite the Orthodox and Catholic communions will never resolve this.

You can see that in a period of eighty years there has been a very active and well-resourced move toward inter-church dialogue. I don't oppose this. However, there is an inbuilt flaw by which, as I have already stated, it is destined to fail.

<u>Seeking an Overlap</u>

First, imagine that we have two Christian denominations, let's call them A and B. And let's say that they broadly overlap in their beliefs and practices. (Fig. 1)

Fig 1.

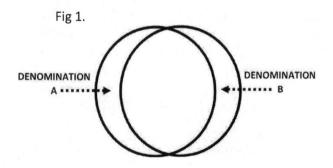

DENOMINATION A

DENOMINATION B

It is quite easy to see that the areas where they are already in agreement are quite large compared to those areas where they disagree. (Fig. 2)

Permit me a point of clarification before we go on. In using the words 'agree' and 'disagree' I am specifically talking about agreement on things beyond the core tenets of the Christian faith.

We will discuss what we mean by such core beliefs in some detail in the next section. For now, let's just say they agree or disagree on things that don't affect whether they are Christian or not.

Fig 2.

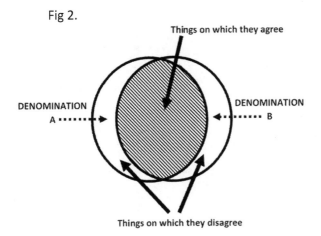

Things on which they agree

DENOMINATION A ••••••→   DENOMINATION ←•••••• B

Things on which they disagree

You could rightly assume that any statement arising from a meeting of these two parts of the Church of Christ would likely be substantive and meaningful and that it would be unlikely that either of them would 'throw their rattle out of the pram'. So far so good.

Now let's consider two other Christian denominations, this time C and D. (Fig. 3)

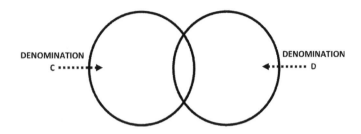

In this case, C and D are very different. They represent very different traditions and histories. Their services, vestments, liturgy, buildings and language are entirely alien to each other. Even a cursory consideration of doctrines shows several potential flashpoints. Consequently, there are few areas on which they readily agree compared to their differences. (Fig 4.)

Fig. 4

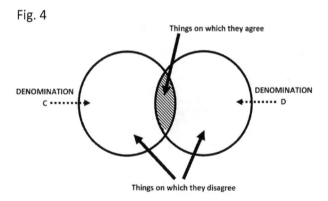

Now the tricky bit. Let's consider a meeting between all four denominations A, B, C and D. Firstly, if we were to impose the large overlap that was agreed between denominations A and B… (Fig 2.) onto the smaller areas of agreement between C and D (Fig 4.) we generate (Fig 5.)

Fig. 5

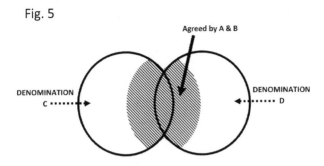

Agreed by A & B

DENOMINATION C

DENOMINATION D

...this would most likely force denomination C and/or D to complain and withdraw.

Alternatively, we could use the points of agreement between C and D but consider it from the perspective of A and B. (Fig 6.)

Fig. 6

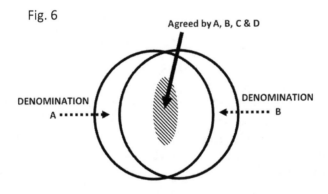

Agreed by A, B, C & D

DENOMINATION A

DENOMINATION B

Can you see how A and B might question whether the small area of overlap was worth the effort.

The Lund Principle

One of the outcomes of the Faith and Order commission of the World Council of Churches is the Lund Principle, named after the Swedish city that hosted their meeting in 1952. The agreed, and now widely adopted, principle states that churches should,

"Act together in all matters except those in which deep differences of conviction compel them to act separately."

The key word that exposes the failing of the Lund Principle is **Act**. In this principal the requirement to 'Act together' is declared as being subservient to 'Differences of Conviction'.

Let me give you a moment to allow that to sink in.

How can the Lund Principle ever be anything more than a statement of defeat? It doesn't demonstrate that we have love one for another, it just shows we are adept at actively avoiding each other! It is predicated on the idea that we care enough about each other not to upset each other. It requires us to whisper anything controversial, as someone might be upset. It gives permission to <u>not</u> act together if we disagree. This cannot be right.

If the principle is that we should act together in the areas we agree, why limit it to just Christian denominations. I am quite happy to act together with the unchurched and even those of other faiths on things that don't matter. What the world is looking for is an active demonstration of Christ's sacrificial love amongst His people. If they were to see opposing factions (and I choose that word specifically) of the Church co-operating with each other, giving space for each other, preferring each other in love, it would have a most powerful effect.

I will propose an opposite ideology in Challenge 3: Acting with Demonstrable Unity but please note the emphasis on the word Acting.

The Only Possible Outcomes of Ecumenism

In recent times church leaders have gathered together to agree a common position on contentious subjects including women in leadership and sexuality. Rather than dive headlong into these particular subjects, with their associated strongly held views, let me create a hypothetical (but nonetheless realistic) example.

Let's imagine that a synod of various church leaders was called to agree a common position on, *"Should the church encourage their congregations to be vaccinated?"*

Within that gathering there may be some who are 100% convinced that the global vaccination programme is a work of the devil (or at least the global elite) and if we were to succumb to it, we would be acting out of fear and not faith. On the other hand, there may be those who are 100% convinced that we have a duty to protect our members (particularly the vulnerable ones) from harm. And then there will be the majority who don't have a strongly held position either way. As we have seen, such a gathering can only have one of two outcomes.

a) A common position statement is agreed that is so inane it is effectively meaningless, such as,

"The church believes that vaccinations are a good thing except when they are not, or your personal beliefs prevent you from partaking."

(I am exaggerating for effect, but you get the idea), or

b) A common position statement is agreed by all except those with a strong contra-position who, at best abstain or more likely leave in a wave of bad-tempered publicity.

You don't need an advanced degree to see that these are the only two outcomes on the 'Common position of the Church' especially on such hyper-contentious subjects. Add to this, a baseload of presently dormant but equally contentious issues across a wide spectrum of current subjects including: The Gifts of the Holy Spirit, The Social Gospel, Alcohol, Race and Class. Then there are also the painful issues that surfaced post-Reformation including: trans-substantiation, predestination, the separation of the clergy and the laity, church governance, and the separation of the Church and State. And finally, there are the divisive doctrinal issues that framed the first three hundred years of the Church on matters of Christology (the nature of Christs divinity), The Eucharist, Baptism and the Hebraic roots of the Church.

The two theoretical outcomes I have described were the actual outcome of the ecumenical debates, meetings and synods that drove a wedge between the Messianic, Coptic, Orthodox, Catholic, Lutheran, Calvinist, Anglican, Baptist and Puritan movements over the last two millennia; a separation that whilst now cold in history, at the time was nonetheless equally as ferocious.

Why do we put ourselves through this?

Acceptance not Standardisation

Ecumenicalism cannot work. Let me clarify what I mean by that. The intention to bring together disparate denominations for the purpose of agreeing a common position on a difficult subject can only produce one of the two outcomes already presented.

As worthy as the Ecumenical goal appears on face value, I hope you can see the inbuilt flaw of standardisation. In fact, I would go as far as to suggest the exact opposite. That the Church needs to embrace its differences. Rather than trying to reach agreement, we need to be able to accept each other's alternative views. In short, we need to **agree to love each other – not agree with each other**.

The One Church is a body made up of many members. If we consider the human body, we see that not only do many parts look and feel very different. Some of them are the exact opposites of the other. A right hand, a right foot and a right nostril are the exact opposites of their left counterparts, are they not? Why can we not accept the fact that one church will be anti-vax (to use my example) whilst another will be pro-vax, and at the same time resist the temptation to define one or other as being right or wrong. **There is no right or wrong – just right and left**.

I know it will be hard to embrace such a stance, as on each subject we will have our own sometimes fiercely held positions. It is these convictions that will rightly drive where you and I fit and which congregations we attend. But, if we slip into avoiding those with alternative positions even on these most reactionary subjects, we will not be acting in love.

Embracing difference is God's heart. That is why he gave us the church-is-a-body metaphor. If we acknowledge that we are a body, His Body, we must accept that we are full of differences, whilst at the same time being precisely <u>one</u> body – precisely One Church.

To do so allows us to move in the opposite spirit from which the world has come to expect from us and will demonstrate that we do after all, *'have love one for another.'*[1]

---

[1] John 13 v 35

7. God's Faithful Remnant

Within the One Church there is a lot of variety. Many denominations, many congregations. That doesn't take a lot of imagination. But in accepting that these differences are something we must actively embrace can be very hard, almost impossible, for some to countenance.

Consider when Paul wrote to the church in Galatia, when addressing specific divisions in gender (male or female), race (Jew or gentile) and social standing (slave or free) he concluded that we are *'All one in Christ Jesus.'*[1] We, of course, know that he wasn't directing this message towards just that church in Galatia, but it is a timeless principle. We are all one in Christ Jesus, and not just in an ethereal sense, but in a down-to-earth hands-on sense that the outside world could tangibly see, and in so doing be drawn to serve Him.

If therefore we accept that we are all one in Christ Jesus, then that has to include every member of the Christian Church. We will tackle the exact definition of the Christian Church in the next section, but it will include those beyond our own theological, doctrinal comfort-zone. It will include, let's be candid, the disagreeable ones.

For some, this is quite frankly too big a conceptual hurdle to overcome and as a consequence an alternative doctrine has surfaced, that of God's Faithful Remnant.

The idea of considering a particular part of the Church to be the Faithful Remnant really became popular in the 1950s when both the Anglican and Roman Catholic communion started using the terminology to rationalise the small numbers of believers that were active in their parishes in the post-war period. In the face of dwindling church attendance, to consider that the small numbers

---

[1] Galatians 3 v 28

are really evidence of being part of God's select Remnant, the chosen few, was a powerful ideology. Sadly, it is closer to wishful thinking than sound doctrine.[1] If you are not aware of this philosophy, let me summarise it as follows:

> "God has chosen a small group of Christians to represent Him and do His work. Therefore only a select few truly dedicated Christians are responsible for God's presence on earth and His activity in any particular area. They alone recognise the needs of those around them and try hard to meet them. They don't seek recognition for their work, they are more than willing to lay down themselves and their families for the sake of the gospel. They work well or even thrive under this pressure and constantly feel burdened to do more knowing one day they will get their reward."

Don't get me wrong, I am a great supporter of sacrificial service. The Church does need to respond to the needs of those around and in God's love seek to meet them. But it is the implied isolationism that concerns me, particularly if it leads to a belief of being the only ones left to fight the good fight.

Origins of the Term

Considering themselves as God's faithful Remnant has been used as a badge of honour for several marginalised parts of the Church. For example, in 1688 when a split happened in the Church of England due to the need to swear the Oath of Allegiance to the new monarch King William, those who refused to comply termed themselves 'The Faithful Remnant of the True Church of England.[2]

---

[1] "The remnant: Biblical reality of wishful thinking?" By Goldstein, Clifford (1994). Perspectives in Religious Studies

[2] 'The Faithful Remnant of the True Church of England': Susanna Hopton and the Politico-Theology of the Nonjuring Schism, Simon Lewis The Journal of Theological Studies, 7/1/2021

The denomination (though they would not term themselves as such) that has been most pivotal in developing Remnant theology, and who apply this as a major tenet of their beliefs and practices is the Brethren movement. Since its foundation in the late 1820s many of its scholars have unequivocally upheld the doctrine that considers itself to be "the Christian remnant in the midst of Christendom's ruins."[1] Consequently, there is an inbuilt tendency to hold themselves apart from other denominations, otherwise the logic of that teaching collapses. This philosophy is enforced within their Assemblies (as they term their congregations) especially the Exclusive ones although, to be fair, their so-called Open Assemblies do find areas to cooperate with a select group of other evangelically focused congregations, with whom they consider there is a like-mindedness.

It is interesting also to note that it is this very movement that popularised the idea of the pre-tribulation rapture of the Church. Forgive me if this terminology if not familiar to you, this is after all a book on church unity not on the book of Revelation. In short, pre-tribulation rapture is the theory that the Church will be whisked-away up to heaven at the start of Act One of the end-time saga. The link between pre-tribulation rapture and remnant philosophy is obvious. If you believe you are part of a very minor, very special remnant, clinging on in the midst of an unbelieving world and an equally apostate church, it is comforting to believe that any-day-now Christ will come and rescue you (and only you). This book is not the forum for a full discussion on this subject, all I am pointing out is the strong co-dependent link between remnant philosophy and that of a pre-tribulation rapture.

Sadly, remnant philosophy has been a theme picked up by several pseudo-Christian sects purporting to be the only true way, most notably Seventh Day Adventists. More on them later.

---

[1] The Remnant — Past and Present by C.H. Mackintosh extracted from brethrenarchive.org

Biblical Basis of Gods Remnant

Despite the obvious attractiveness of the comfort of being the faithful remnant, the idea is entirely at odds with the theology of the remnant we read in scripture which was exclusively about the purification of the Jewish nation. The word remnant was not even in the Hebraic vocabulary until the nation had been so disobedient that God allowed them to be taken captive into Babylon. God's covenant with Abraham meant He would not abandon them and His eternal love for His nation led Him to assure them that despite all that they had done, He would not abandon them and would bring some of them back to their homeland.

> 'And it shall come to pass in that day that the _remnant_ of Israel, and such as have escaped of the house of Jacob, will never again depend on him who defeated them, but will depend on the Lord, the Holy One of Israel, in truth. The _remnant_ will return, the _remnant_ of Jacob, to the Mighty God. For though your people, O Israel, be as the sand of the sea, a _remnant_ of them will return.'[1]

Nehemiah, Ezra, Haggai and Zechariah all use the term remnant to describe those who returned from captivity.

The Jewish people have clung to the same remnant promise over the centuries since the fall of the nation in AD73. It has been a promise that sustained them throughout the subsequent occupations by Byzantine, Crusader, Mamluk, Ottoman and British forces until independence in 1948. But this is not part of our study.

The remnant was that part of the Israel nation which God preserved in order to maintain His covenant with Abraham. The Old Testament teaching is clear. Return from captivity = Remnant. But what of the New Testament?

---

[1] Isaiah 10 vs 20-23

There are two passages in the New Testament that reference the Remnant. The first is in the book of Romans the second in the book of Revelation.

Firstly, Romans chapters 9 to 11 concern Israel's rejection of Christ and how that rejection is not total as God has preserved a remnant from within the Jewish nation. The key passage being in chapter 11.

'I say then, has God cast away His people? Certainly not! For I also am an Israelite, of the seed of Abraham, of the tribe of Benjamin. God has not cast away His people whom He foreknew ... Even so then, at this present time there is a <u>remnant</u> according to the election of grace...What then? Israel has not obtained what it seeks; but the elect have obtained it, and the rest were blinded.'[1]

Here Paul uses the term remnant to describe the elect, or those who have accepted the saving grace of Jesus. He points out that whilst Israel has not obtained 'what it seeks' i.e. the Messiah, there is a remnant from within the Jews that have accepted Jesus as their Messiah. Those from within the Jewish faith that have accepted Jesus (or Yeshua as they would call him) and put their faith in his atoning sacrifice, we call Messianic Jews. This term includes not only Paul himself but the vast majority of the population of the Church in existence at the time of the New Testament's writing. This would have been true even in Rome which despite its distance from Judea nonetheless had a large Jewish enclave, in the middle of the city, on the right bank of the Tiber.

In Romans chapter 11 Paul then goes on to compare this remnant with Elijah. When the Old Testament prophet thought he was alone and the only faithful one left, God responded that there were seven thousand others waiting in reserve who also had not bowed the knee to Baal. The parallel is quite striking. Elijah had to accept that there was a vast number of equally faithful souls, and

---

[1] Romans 11 vs 1,2a,5,7

he wasn't the only faithful one. Similarly, the Messianic converts that Paul was writing to, needed to make room for what became the much larger number of gentile converts to the same faith. We see the outworking of this throughout the book of Acts.

The second New Testament reference is in Revelation,

'And the dragon was enraged with the woman, and he went to make war with <u>the rest of</u> her offspring, who keep the commandments of God and have the testimony of Jesus Christ.' [1]

In the imagery of Revelation, the *'woman'* is Israel. In this passage the phrase *'the rest of'* (in some versions remnant) are once again those who *'have the testimony of Jesus Christ'*, once again we see it refers to the Messianic Jews.

Neither of these New Testament references relate to the Church, let alone the state of the end-time Church. Both are about the preservation of the nation of Israel, through Messianic believers.

<u>Being Grafted in</u>

The New Testament makes it abundantly clear that gentile believers are grafted into the remnant of Israel (i.e. the Messianic believers) or as Paul describes it, the holy root.[2] Paul makes it clear that only a part of Israel has been blinded[3] and God is able to graft any Jew who puts their faith in Yeshua back into the One Church.[4]

It is essential to understand that the gentile church has not replaced Israel in God's affections. This is a very false teaching that has invaded the Church through the heresy of Marcion of Sinope in the late first century; a heresy for which he was summarily excommunicated by every bishop at the time. And yet

---

[1] Revelation 12 v 17
[2] Romans 11 v 16
[3] Romans 11 v 25
[4] Romans 11 v 23

his heresy took hold and eventually has become a core belief of much of the Church, even to today.

This is not the forum to explore that doctrine in detail, but I hope I have presented it in sufficient detail to allow you to accept that Jesus isn't returning for a remnant, a handful of faithful souls scattered across an apostate church landscape. He is returning for a glorious and spotless global bride.

I did hear an analogy presented many years ago by a preacher, forgive but me I can't remember his name, but he was talking about the parable of the wheat and the tares.[1] Which to remind you tells of a wheat field contaminated with tares, a weed that looks like wheat. The parable goes on to say that it would be near impossible to separate out the two crops until harvest at which point the weeds could be removed and burned, allowing the wheat to be separated out and used. The preacher made the point, and it has stuck with me for years, that it was a wheat field, not a weed field. Despite the contamination the wheat was in the ascendancy. I think this is a good point, well made. Surely Jesus would have given a different parable if he had needed to describe the harvesting of a small handful of wheat stalks, clinging on for survival, in the midst of an enormous and overpowering field full of weeds.

To remind you, we are looking at the need to dismantle the structures of disunity. Remnant theology is part of that but perhaps not for the majority. Nonetheless it is important to root out and discard any belief that even hints to exclusivism that would falsely claim that our own expression of church is the only one. Such an ideology can never represent Christ's all-encompassing love to a fallen world.

---

[1] Matthew 13:24-30

8. Denominational and Apostolic Alignment

The final structure we need to dismantle is a bit more controversial. So far, we have looked at the Church Universal vs Church Local idea; Ecumenism and Remnant Theology but in this chapter, we will be taking an axe to the very roots of our perceived identity.

How do you describe yourself as a Christian? If someone asks you, "What sort of Christian are you?" How would you answer. How do you describe your church?

As we now are beginning to explore the idea that there is just One Church and that every congregation is an essential part of it, it begs the question 'Where do denominations fit in Biblically?' Let's take it a step further. There is a growing trend amongst independent charismatic congregations to be 'aligned' with specific so-called Apostolic or Prophetic ministries. Whilst such alignment is voluntary it nonetheless promotes the modern-day Apostle or Prophet to a governmental role not dissimilar to that of an Archbishop in a traditional episcopal church. The words might differ, but the role remains much the same.

Is there a Biblical basis for such denominational (including alignment) identification within the One Church ideology? Let's take a look.

As a starting point let's consider all of the churches listed in the New Testament. There are several. Those to whom Paul's epistles were written obviously jump out, as do the seven churches that appear at the beginning of Revelation. But if you dig a little further no less than 39 specific identifiable churches are documented in the New Testament. For completeness, I have listed them all as follows:

New Testament Churches

Firstly, those linked to a specific city:
1. Antioch, Pisidia: Acts 13:14; Gal 1:2
2. Antioch, Syria: Acts 11:26
3. Athens: Acts 17:34
4. Babylon: 1 Peter 5:13
5. Berea: Acts 17:11
6. Caesarea: Acts 10:1 & 48
7. Cenchrea: Rom 16:1
8. Colossae: Col 1:2
9. Corinth: Acts 18:1
10. Crete: Titus 1:5
11. Cyrene: Acts 11:20
12. Damascus: Acts 9:19
13. Derbe: Acts 14:20; Gal 1:2
14. Ephesus: Acts 18:19, Rev 1:11
15. Hierapolis Col 4:13
16. Iconium: Acts 14:1; Gal 1:2
17. Jerusalem: Acts 2:5
18. Joppa: Acts 9:36, 38
19. Laodicea: Rev 1:11, Col 4:15
20. Lydda: Acts 9:32
21. Lystra: Acts 14:6; Gal 1:2
22. Pergamum: Rev 1:11
23. Philadelphia: Rev 1:11
24. Philippi: Acts 16:12
25. Puteoli, Italy: Acts 28:13-14
26. Rome: Rom 1:7
27. Sardis: Rev 1:11
28. Sharon: Acts 9:35
29. Smyrna: Rev 1:11
30. Tarsus: Acts 9:30
31. Thessalonica: Acts 17:1
32. Thyatira: Rev 1:11; Acts 16:14
33. Troas: Acts 20:6-7

Then there are several churches that lie across a region:
34. Asia: 1 Cor 16:19
35. Galatia: Gal 1:2
36. Judea: Gal 1:22
37. Macedonia: 2 Cor 8:1
38. Phoenicia: Acts 11:19
39. Samaria: Acts 8:14, 25

It doesn't take much to work out that all of these churches are exclusively named after the place (either a city or a region) where they are located.

Does this mean that there should be just one church in each geographical area? Well, as far as God is concerned, perhaps there already is just One Church in each of our cities and regions.

It is only when we insist on putting a label on each congregation (e.g. Baptist, Methodist, Catholic, etc.) that we then consider it as somehow disconnected from the other congregations in the vicinity. This mentality is completely at odds with the way the Church was described in the New Testament let alone the specific prayer of our Lord in Gethsemane where He twice prayed, *'That they may be one'*.[1]

But isn't it oversimplistic to say that in the very early days of the Church that geography was the only factor? Well, let's look at what happened when differences in interpretation and practice entered the frame.

<u>Paul and Apollos</u>

Let us consider Paul's first letter to the church in Corinth where he makes the observation that some members of the Corinthian church considered themselves to be *'of Apollos'* whereas others identified themselves as being *'of Paul.'*[2] Clearly there was a distinction in the minds of the congregants that there was a difference. Whether it was the teaching, ethos, style, personality, or just that they made their commitment to Christ under these two respective Apostles (or to use the Latin, missionaries), we will never know. But what is clear is that there was the seed of division. Without Paul's sharp and early intervention, we would probably read in the New Testament

---

[1] John 17 vs 11 & 21
[2] 1 Corinthians 3 v 4

about the two churches in that city: The Pauline Church of Corinth and The Corinthian Church of Apollos.

Apollos was a great preacher and teacher whom God used mightily to bring many Jews to faith in Christ. Hailing from Alexandria he is known to have initially preached only *'The Baptism of John.'*[1] By this we can infer that his preaching was mainly about repentance and that the Jews should return to God, by placing their faith in the Messiah. Paul, on the other hand, taught more of what we would today call living a Christian lifestyle empowered by the Holy Spirit. There is nothing wrong with the teaching of Apollos; indeed for many churches today this is the sole intent of their mission, and they are very good at it. I grew up in a congregation that preached a gospel service every Sunday evening regardless that there were no visitors in the building at all. They were, quite literally, preaching to the converted. But that was the mission of that particular congregation and I honour them for their faithfulness in it.

Looking more into Apollos we see that Priscilla and Aquila were the ones who helped open Apollos' eyes to the fulness of the gospel whilst they were at Ephesus.[2] A little later in Acts we then see how prevalent Apollos' foundational teaching was to the church at Ephesus.

'And he said to them, "Did you receive the Holy Spirit when you believed?" And they said, "No, we have not even heard that there is a Holy Spirit." And he said, "Into what then were you baptized?" They said, "Into John's baptism." And Paul said, "John baptized with the baptism of repentance, telling the people to believe in the one who was to come after him, that is, Jesus." On hearing this, they were baptized in the name of the Lord Jesus. And when Paul had laid his hands on them, the Holy Spirit came on them, and they began speaking in tongues and prophesying.'[3]

---

[1] Acts 18 v 25
[2] Acts 18 v 26
[3] Acts 19 vs 2-6

If, for a moment, we look at extra-Biblical historical texts we discover that Apollos became so dissatisfied with the division at Corinth that by the time of Paul's letter he had already left and retired to Crete with Zenas. After Paul's intervention healed the schism, Apollos returned and became one of the elders of the Corinthian church.

So much for the Apollos bio, but the important bit is to see how Paul, in his Letter to Corinth, confronted this Apollos/Paul divide. He gave a message of healing which managed to bring together two groups that followed two different people with two subtly different doctrines.

Paul's message was clear and forthright.

'For when one says, "I am of Paul," and another, "I am of Apollos," are you not carnal?' [1]

That is not pulling any punches. When you say you are aligned with one Leader or Apostle or Evangelist at the expense of the other, then you are being carnal or worldly. He goes on to explain to his readers,

'I planted, Apollos watered, but God gave the increase.'

He makes the point that different external ministries have a different purpose, perhaps at different times, on the development and growth of any particular congregation. He planted - Apollos watered.

'Who then is Paul, and who is Apollos, but ministers through whom you believed, as the Lord gave to each one?' [2]

Paul stresses that when he addresses the church at Corinth, he is just 'doing his job,' (Well, doing his 'calling' more accurately) and that was true of Apollos also, whom we can

---

[1] 1 Corinthians 3 v 4
[2] 1 Corinthians 3 v 5

79

assume he considered a fellow worker, not a rival. At no point does he claim that the church at Corinth belonged to him, nor for that matter to Apollos. Despite the problems in Corinth, at no time in his writings did he threaten to dismiss the local leaders as that was not within his power nor part of his mission. He advised and chastised but that was as far as he could go. How different is this to the relationship we see between individual congregations and external ministry, be they Episcopal, Apostolic or otherwise, which are often based on conformity, allegiance and identity.

Paul then goes even further to completely devalue what both he and Apollos had brought,

'So then neither he who plants is anything, nor he who waters, but God who gives the increase.'[1]

If I may paraphrase, in short, he simply says, "Picking sides is wrong because neither of us is worth it." Can you get a sense of the disarming power with which he intervenes in this dangerously developing rift? And then as if to drive the point home he delivers the killer punch,

'Now he who plants, and he who waters are one,'[2]

Please, don't miss this. This is a huge statement which is so easily overlooked. Here we see the very first written response on how to deal with a serious division in a church. And in his response, we read Paul categorically say... **there may be practical differences, but we are still one**.

It's All About Geography

We can see that whilst there were slight differences in the teaching, from the various Apostles and preachers in the

---

[1] 1 Corinthians 3 v 7
[2] 1 Corinthians 3 v 8

New Testament, nonetheless the only differences between churches were geographic.

This is, of course, the opposite of today where I find that I am in the catchment of a great number of potential congregations. In fact, if I consider that it's not unreasonable to travel say 30 mins to attend a Sunday service, I have the option of attending over a hundred different congregations.

So, does that mean I am advocating that all of the churches within a specific local geography should amalgamate? That there should be just one church in each town, city or region?

It would be all too easy for me to say no. That since the first century things have changed irrevocably. I could say that the reality of today's situation is fundamentally different and pragmatically we need to recognise the near impossibility of such a bold move. However, to accept the status quo would put me at odds with how God patently views His Church. It would also undermine the whole premise of this book! Let me say it again. We are One Church. Acting as multiple is at odds with His truth. Whether we like it or not Jesus is coming back for One Bride not 22,400.

But I am not advocating mass amalgamation. We are different for a very wonderful and powerful reason as we will see shortly.

Let's not get too downhearted at the enormity of this task. Thankfully God has given us clear instruction at how we can consider His One Church as a single entity whilst accepting that there are certain (sometimes dramatic) differences within it. That is exactly what we will tackle in the rest of this book starting with the very real issue of disagreements on doctrine.

Challenge 2: Dealing with Differences

9. But I Just Cannot Agree with Them!

There is a lot of diversity across the Christian Church. I guess that is a big understatement. With the vast number of denominations and rites it is inevitable that there will be a lot of variety. Let's take a detailed look at this to see if we can identify the causes of schism.

Imagine that we took a sheet of paper and wrote on it the practices of a denomination. By that I mean, how they conduct their services, how they are organised, etc. Having done this, we then take another sheet and do the same for a second denomination, and so on. Perhaps not all of them, maybe just sticking to the major ones. Then we laid out these sheets of paper on a table side-by-side and, using a coloured highlighter, began to mark the areas of difference. We would quickly have a very colourful table, but then various repeating themes would emerge. What we would find is something like the areas of difference that I have listed on the next couple of pages. Whilst these differences are confined to practices, rather than doctrinal beliefs, several of them have nonetheless been the cause of historical church schism and in some cases bloodshed. Let's not be too dismissive of differences in practice.

But this isn't just a list for reference; it is an opportunity, to explore how differing church practices sit with you. You will see that I have framed each point as a question, and I am making no judgement as to what the correct answers are to those questions. If you are willing, as you read through the list, answer each question to reflect your own beliefs. There is no score system at the end, and you won't suddenly find out that you are in the wrong denomination, but I would like you to do the mental (or is it spiritual) exercise to consider every question on its own merit.

I am then going to ask you to run down the list a second time, but more of that in a moment.

The Christian Difference Engine

The Worship Service
- Should a service be led by a specific leader, or can anyone do it?
- Can a service happen anywhere or only in a church building?
- Should it happen weekly, daily or just whenever convenient?
- Which of the following are acceptable forms of corporate worship?
  - Singing
  - Dancing
  - Chanting
  - Silence
  - Prayer
  - Speaking in tongues
  - Reading from the Bible
  - Reciting a written liturgy
  - Reciting it in a foreign language (e.g. Latin)
  - Lighting of a candle
  - Looking at an inspired work of art
  - Kissing (i.e. a kiss of peace on the cheek)
  - Almsgiving
  - Partaking in The Eucharist

The Eucharist
- Does it matter what we call the sacramental remembrance?
- Who should administer the sacraments?
- What type of bread is to be eaten? Same regarding the cup?
- Can it be taken anywhere or only in a church building?
- How frequently, should it be taken?
- Do you need to fast prior to participating, as well as abstaining from other pleasures?
- Can people who are not members of the congregation or denomination participate equally?

Baptism
- Is it for the dedication of children or the testimony of adults? or both?
- Should one be fully emersed or sprinkled on the forehead?
- Should there be a single baptism, or can it be repeated?
- Who should conduct the baptism?

Prayer
- You can pray at any time but is it helpful to have special times of day to pray?
- Can prayers be recited from a text, or must they come spontaneously from within? Or either?
- Can prayers be sung or be silent?

Governance
- Are some Christians called to be leaders over others? Or are all Christians equal?
- What should a leader be called? Bishop, Elder, Priest, Pastor, Father, Vicar, Leader or doesn't it matter?
- Is church leadership only for men?
- Should a church be led by a single individual or a team?
- Should leaders dress differently, especially when conducting a worship service?
- Should the leader(s) of a congregation be accountable to someone outside the congregation?
- Should there be a denominational hierarchy?
- If there is a church hierarchy, should the top be an individual or a team?

Holy Days
- Are some days in the year more special (or Holy) than others?
- Is it important to mark the dates of Christ's birth as well as His crucifixion and resurrection? Does it matter which days we use?

Food & Drink
- Should Christians abstain from certain foods?
- Is total abstinence from alcohol important?
- Should Christians fast? If so, when? Are there special fasting times of year?

Confession
- Is confessing our sins a personal and private matter, or something we should do with another trusted person?

Saints
- Are all Christians called saints or just the notable ones?
- Is it acceptable to honour a Christian on a certain day? Even a notable one from history?

Good Works
- Is the fact that a Christian performs good works evidence (i.e. fruit) of their salvation?

I am not suggesting that the above list is definitive, but it does cover the majority of differences in practice and form that you are likely to find across most denominations.

If you did humour me by considering each question honestly then thank you. Having now attested to your own beliefs, I would now like you to go down the list a second time. But this time consider the <u>opposite</u> answers to the ones you chose. As you do, ask yourself the following question. "If I met someone who claimed to be a Christian and yet held the opposite viewpoint to my own, would I consider them to be a Christian or not?"

Of course, being a Christian is a personal thing and not just to do with how they behave, but they are, to some extent, interrelated and it is all too easy to confuse the two. Indeed, church history has taught us that the norm has been to define a Christian expressly by their activity during a worship service rather than their personal faith. That is one of the very problems that has gotten us into the 22,400-denominational mess. So, this is where we need to start. Again, this only works if you are honest with yourself. I'll give you a minute or two to complete your second run through.

I am hoping that you found nothing that was a dealbreaker. Despite the wide diversity of practice, it is my hope that nothing on the list would prompt you to question Mr Opposite's faith. After all, that is God's prerogative not ours!

Let's not forget that Christianity is about personal faith, not corporate practice. It is based on the "belief in and acceptance of the death and resurrection of Jesus, sinful humans are thereby offered salvation, and the promise of eternal life." At least that is the definition from The Oxford Companion to the Bible[1] (it is also the one that millions will read on Wikipedia), but we are getting ahead of ourselves. The only point I am trying to make here is that

---

[1] Wikipedea.com/Christianity quoting Metzger/Coogan, Oxford Companion to the Bible, pp. 513, 649.

the list of church practices we went through a few moments ago were just that – practices. None of them should have any bearing on our salvation. We will return to the definition of what makes a Christian shortly.

So, that is an important foundation laid. We could attend a congregation whose practices were the complete opposite to your personal preference, and yet stand shoulder to shoulder with our fellow brothers and sisters in Christ. That is a great start – albeit an easy one. I wouldn't be surprised if you're already one step ahead of me. It isn't about what we <u>do</u> that divides us, it is about what we <u>believe</u>. That is true, but don't overlook the importance of accepting differences of performance, practice and style. As I said earlier some of these differences have caused real division in the past.

Core Truth

I had a really useful conversation with someone recently on the subject of how congregations can be united despite having differing views on various doctrines. By doctrine I mean the beliefs, instructions, principles or positions that are held by a denomination; sometimes this is termed its Catechism. The person with whom I was talking had a firmly held belief that there are three categories, or levels, of importance, into which any doctrinal issue could be assigned. He termed these as <u>Primary</u>, <u>Secondary</u> and <u>Tertiary</u> issues. I asked him for a definition of these terms.

The first one was reasonably straightforward. "A Primary issue," he said, "was something that was essential for salvation," and quoted examples such as the omniscience of God the Father, the divinity of Christ and the atoning sacrifice of calvary. I couldn't disagree, in fact, I would go as far as to say if a congregation or denomination does not share the Core Truths of the Christian faith, they are not a Christian entity, are not part of His Body, and as such we are not *'members one of another'*[1]. Note however that this situation does not preclude individuals within such a non-Christian organisation from finding faith in Christ. Those who seek Him will find Him.[2]

We will return to his definitions of Secondary and Tertiary issues in a moment, but first let's stick with Primary issues, or rather Core Truths. The difficulty, of course, is the question: "What is the list of core truths?" or more accurately "Whose list do we use?"

The infallibility of scripture is the only place we look, "Solo Scriptura" as Martin Luther would have put it. If it is in the Bible, then it is fact. This is the most important foundation the Church is built upon.

Pragmatically, though we must admit that this single foundation has nonetheless resulted in many very different structures to have been built upon it. Does this mean there is ambiguity in scripture? Does this mean that the Core Truths (the so-called Primary Issues) are open to debate? Surely not!

To attempt to understand the basis of the Core Truths of the Christian faith we need to go back in time... a long way back in time to the first three centuries of the life of the Church where this issue was first addressed.

The Apostolic Fathers

In the period following Jesus' ascension, all eyes fell on the Apostles to explain the tenets of this new version of Judaism, initially called The Way, but which would become known as Christianity. During this so-called Apostolic period no one was in any doubt as to what to believe and as the Church expanded, several of those Apostles committed their beliefs to paper, or

---

[1] Romans 12 v 5
[2] See 1 Chronicles 28 v 9

more accurately to parchment or papyrus. We have the writings of four of them: Matthew, Peter, Paul and John, included within the canon of the New Testament. As important as these writings are, the Apostles also spent much of their ministry mentoring and teaching others. Their disciples had first-hand experience of Apostolic instruction and, we can safely assume, were equally as sure of what they believed. We call these 'second generation' ministers the Apostolic Fathers, and they lived over the period of around AD50 to 150. They are those with extensive personal first-hand knowledge of the Apostles and who learned their faith directly from them. Several wrote down what they learned and, again, some of those writings are included within the New Testament. The writings of Mark, Luke, Jude and probably James (some scholars disagree) resulted from the teaching that overflowed from the Apostles whom they knew intimately well, plus of course the divine inspiration of the Holy Spirit, and are:

"*Living and powerful, and sharper than any two-edged sword, piercing even to the division of soul and spirit, and of joints and marrow, and is a discerner of the thoughts and intents of the heart.*"[1]

But they are not the only Apostolic Fathers who wrote extensively during the early life of the Church. Others, whose works survive to this day, include Clement of Rome, Ignatius of Antioch and Polycarp of Smyrna, each one the leader of a church mentioned in the New Testament. Their writings are not accepted as canonical, which means they are not considered as inspired. Whilst the style and subject matter is very similar to the letters of Paul, they are evidently not the word of God. That being said, their writings can nonetheless be useful to help us gain an understanding of what the Church was like in that period, especially if we avoid focusing on just one author or text. We can treat their observations as historical fact though not gospel truth, a subtle yet very important difference.

---

[1] Hebrews 4 v 12

For example, we discover that the church in a given city or geographic region whilst being run by elders was overseen by a bishop. We also see that they conversed with each other so as to keep each other on the right path and agree a united response to challenges, controversies and heresy.

There were a number of major heretical challenges during the early Church period, (some of which I shall cover in detail later) but despite the heresy and the early Church's extensive geographic spread, and despite the absence of any living Apostles, nor the written New Testament, despite all of these obstacles the entire Church was completely united. Everyone believed the same thing. In the words of the travelling church chronicler Hegesippus (AD110-180), "In each city all is according to the ordinances of the law and the Prophets and the Lord." [1]

The Ante-Nicene Church Fathers

Winding the clock forward, we then enter a period where these Apostolic Fathers passed the baton on to the next generation. Now we have church overseers, the bishops, whose understanding of the gospel and the Christian faith has been imbibed through personal relationship with the Apostolic Fathers, who themselves sat under the ministry of the Apostles.

For example, Irenaeus (AD130-202) learned directly from Polycarp of Smyrna, who learned directly from the Apostle John. Sadly, for most of the others the direct spiritual ancestry is less easy to document. Several of the more notable church leaders of this era hailed from Alexandria where, according to tradition and historical evidence, the church was founded by Mark, the author of the gospel.

We call the church leaders and writers who lived in the period between AD150 to AD300 the Ante-Nicene Church Fathers.

---

[1] Eusebius, Church History iv 22

Ante- meaning 'before' and 'Nicene' referencing the Council of Nicaea which is the ultimate goal of this short history lesson.

Once again, many of these bishops (and some of the elders) were great writers, especially those who were motivated to make written defences (or Apologies) against new heretical challenges during that period. Much of their writings survive to this day. Some of the more well-known Ante-Nicene apologists are:

Irenaeus (AD130-202)
Clement of Alexandria (AD150-255)
Tertullian (AD155-220)
Hippolytus of Rome (AD170-235)
Origen (AD185-254)
Dionysius of Alexandria (AD200-265)
Cyprian of Carthage (AD200-258)
Gregory Thaumaturgus (AD213-270)

The writings of this group, often termed the Apologists, again offer us important historical insights into the Church of the period. However, we can assume that as we are now two-generations from the Apostles, differences in understanding have begun to get some traction. And yet the Church is still united.

By the end of the third century there were a reported 1800 Christian bishops across the Roman empire, and we can add to that number those in Ethiopia, Arabia, India and beyond. We considered what the early Church looked like in a previous chapter, but for now let's just focus on the number. Some scholars have stated that the total number of congregations at that time probably exceeded 10,000. All of these were held together through personal relationships, frequent discourse and the grace of the Holy Spirit.

Let that sink in. There was no hierarchy, no area committees or national synods. Each church was overseen by a bishop, who was in relationship with, and on an equal level with, his neighbouring bishops. In time there was a growing recognition that the five bishops who led the congregations at Rome, Antioch, Constantinople, Alexandria and Jerusalem were more senior than the rest. Yet these five, who eventually would become known as Patriarchs, had no direct authority over any other bishop, as was evidenced in the writings of Clement of Rome who offered words of encouragement and counsel to the wayward congregation at Corinth (yes, Corinth again!), rather than exercising any authority to bring them in line.

But to say that the Church remained perfectly uniform at this point in time would be an oversimplification. The sheer scale of the Church meant that it was beginning to creak and buckle as differences, though not divisions, began to surface.

Before we get to the Council of Nicaea, we need to look at how the Church dealt with several pagan philosophies that began to seep into the Church, and which some 'rogue' bishops began to teach. Over the first three centuries there were quite few.

The Gnostic Heresy

The first heresy that challenged the infant Church was Gnosticism which became prevalent across many parts of Europe from the late first century. I won't go into much detail on the origins or teachings of Gnosticism, rather I want to focus on how the rapidly sprawling Church responded to it. Simplistically it was the belief that the physical world was evil, the unseen/spiritual world was good and that the spiritual part within us all needs to be liberated through special knowledge (Greek: Gnosis). There are echoes of this within modern New Age philosophy and conspiracy theories.

Several Apologists, including Tertullian and Hippolytus, wrote against the Gnostic philosophy and their writings were circulated widely. But it was Irenaeus' work 'Adversus Haereses' (or Against Heresies) that was most successful in exposing the errors. In it he used Biblical exposition plus a reliance upon the fact that "The Church... received from the Apostles and their disciples its faith." In so doing he emphasised the vital importance of using Apostolic tradition as the plumbline by which to test new teachings against scripture.

No matter how good 'Against Heresies' was, the fact remained that most church members of that era couldn't read. Consequently, there began to circulate a number of easy-to-remember chants, or creeds, that encapsulated the truths of the Christian faith that refuted Gnosticism.

Whilst the first written versions of what we now know as The Apostles' Creed are dated a century or so later, it is widely believed that it came into common use as the principal weapon against Gnosticism. The title 'The Apostle's Creed' does not attest to its authorship, as the Apostles were long dead by then, but rather to the authority of the truths being passed down from the Apostles.

The Apostles' Creed

I believe in God, the Father almighty,
creator of heaven and earth.
I believe in Jesus Christ, His only Son,
our Lord, who was conceived by the Holy Spirit,
born of the Virgin Mary, suffered under Pontius Pilate,
was crucified, died, and was buried;
He descended to the dead (or into Hell);
On the third day He rose again; He ascended into heaven,
He is seated at the right hand of (God) the Father,
and he will come to judge the living and the dead.
I believe in the Holy Spirit, the holy catholic Church,
the communion of saints, the forgiveness of sins,
the resurrection of the body, and the life everlasting.
Amen.

NB Brackets indicate differences between versions in popular use today.

The Marcion Heresy

A second and very damaging heresy surfaced from within Gnosticism. Marcion, the Bishop of Sinope, in Northern Turkey, declared that Christ had not come to fulfil Hebrew prophesy but rather that Christianity had replaced Judaism. Antisemitic Marcion rejected everything Jewish. He concluded that the entire Old Testament must be rejected, plus many of the accepted and widely circulated writings of the Apostles and Apostolic Fathers. He also rejected much of the accepted New Testament and proposed his own stripped-down subset. This is the point when Replacement Theology (or Supersessionism) began.

Many of the church fathers including Irenaeus, Origen and Tertullian rightly denounced him as a heretic. The aged Polycarp even called him "The first born of Satan." Marcion was duly excommunicated from the Church in AD144 and died a few years later.

By implication of the Church's response, we can see that the accepted view at the time was that the Church retained a strong Jewish identity which the church fathers actively defended even though many of them were gentiles. We know from history that many early churches met in synagogues and celebrated the feasts of Passover, Pentecost and Tabernacles.

Sadly, we see that despite his complete denunciation, Marcion's teachings began to take hold to the extent that some persist to this day.

As a direct consequence of his challenge to scripture, steps were then taken to agree which writings were to be included in the canon of the New Testament.

There were several other contentions and heresies that surfaced during the period of the early church fathers, but for brevity I will simply say that they were all dealt with by the united Church closing ranks against any obvious error. Small-scale regional gatherings of bishops were sometimes held to discuss the issues and the Apologists wrote Biblically sound defences.

The Edict of Milan

Things changed fundamentally when we get to the year AD303, when, under the Roman Emperor Diocletian, The Great Persecution against the Christians began. This was the first empire-wide persecution and lasted for ten years until Constantine became the sole Roman Emperor and passed the Edict of Milan (AD313) that not only tolerated Christianity but effectively made it the state religion.

For nearly 300 years the Church had existed as a largely underground organisation that had grown phenomenally despite the active opposition of the state. Its members knew that their faith was to be tested by persecution and in many cases martyrdom. With few exceptions this had been the fate of the Apostles and early church fathers. They set a powerful example of enduring faith.

But now the state, in the form of Emperor Constantine, had aligned itself with the Christian Church rather than against it. For the first time Christianity had become popular, fashionable and de rigueur for those in power. This produced a whole new problem across the world-wide Church – what we might call Nominality as church numbers were swelled by those whose Christianity was in name-only, lacking any personal commitment or faith.

Around this time a fresh heresy sprang up, known as Arianism. Again, I won't go into detail other than to say it related to the belief that Christ's divinity and humanity did not coexist and as such Jesus was not as divine as God the Father. This heresy was no more troubling than the other errors which the multitude of like-minded bishops had dealt with previously. What was now different was that for the first time in history, the bishops were able to physically meet together en-masse to agree their unified response. Indeed, Emperor Constantine insisted that they did so and invited all 1800 to his summer retreat at the resort town of Nicaea.

At the Council of Nicaea (AD325) the latent differences between individual bishops became evident. In addition to the handful that held to the heretical Arian doctrine other tensions and squabbles surfaced. Despite all of this, the principal outcome of the Council was, as you might expect, the Nicene Creed.

The Nicene Creed

The Nicene Creed was the distillation of the Apostles' Creed already in wide circulation, and various other creeds that were memorised and recited by Christian converts at their baptisms. The final wording of the Nicene Creed was fashioned specifically to refute the Arian heresy, that is why there is such an emphasis on the nature of Christ's 'substance'. But what was most notable was that this was the first time a definitive statement of Christian belief had been written down and agreed by everyone. Can we just dwell on that fact for a moment? The Nicene Creed was agreed by <u>everyone</u>. Well, excluding the handful of Arian bishops who were summarily excommunicated.

Every Christian denomination that we have today, whether they call themselves Catholic, Orthodox, Coptic Protestant, Evangelical, Charismatic or something else, can trace their origins to that very day in 325 when the demonstrably united Church agreed. The Nicene Creed is therefore a hugely positive step forward in our quest for a list of Core Truths of the Christian faith.

The Nicene Creed

We believe in one God, the Father Almighty, the maker of heaven and earth, of things visible and invisible.

And in one Lord Jesus Christ, the Son of God, the begotten of God the Father, the only begotten, that is of the essence of the Father.

God of God, Light of Light, true God of true God, begotten and not made; of the very same nature of the Father, by Whom all things came into being, in heaven and on earth, visible and invisible.

Who for us humanity and for our salvation came down from heaven, was incarnate, was made human, was born perfectly of the holy virgin Mary by the Holy Spirit.

By whom He took body, soul, and mind, and everything that is in man, truly and not in semblance.

He suffered, was crucified, was buried, rose again on the third day, ascended into heaven with the same body, [and] sat at the right hand of the Father.

He is to come with the same body and with the glory of the Father, to judge the living and the dead; of His kingdom there is no end.

We believe in the Holy Spirit, in the uncreated and the perfect; Who spoke through the Law, prophets, and Gospels; Who came down upon the Jordan, preached through the apostles, and lived in the saints.

We believe also in only One, Universal, Apostolic, and (Holy) Church; in one baptism in repentance, for the remission, and forgiveness of sins; and in the resurrection of the dead, in the everlasting judgement of souls and bodies, and the Kingdom of Heaven and in the everlasting life

NB Brackets indicate differences between versions in popular use today.

To say that everyone agreed with the outcome of the Council of Nicaea would be to overlook the hugely significant death knell that was sounded immediately after the creed was agreed. Reaching agreement on the creed had been a somewhat bruising encounter. Most of the bishops involved were so emotionally and physically exhausted that despite the protestations of some, most allowed the next item of business to pass through uncontested. What was the second agenda item? On face value it may look like a minor agreement, but in fact it was a hugely significant shift.

In addition to writing the Nicene Creed to refute the Arian heresy, the Council of Nicaea reached an agreement on the date on which the Church would mark the Crucifixion and Resurrection. Prior to that point the congregations in the East celebrated it on the Biblical feast of Passover; just as the Apostle John, Polycarp, Irenaeus and others had taught them. But in the West, it had moved to be marked on the first day of the week, the Sunday, closest to Passover. At Nicaea the Church sided with the Western (i.e. Roman) patriarchy and what we now call Easter (it wasn't actually called that in those days) became the norm. This decision was a lot more than agreeing a date. Despite the clear defence made by the Apostolic fathers (particularly against Marcion one hundred and eighty years prior), there was no more fight left in the room and by the passing of a simple motion the Church was formally separated from its Jewish heritage.

Have you ever considered, not what is in the Nicene Creed but rather what is missing from it? It fails to mention: the Sabbath, God's appointed feasts of Passover, Pentecost and Tabernacles, the Hebraic (Old Testament) Scriptures, God's covenant with Abraham and the coming of the New Jerusalem. Some would say that these are not Core Truths, but of course, others would disagree pointing out that the Christian Church is the fulfilment of Old Testament prophecy, not the start of an alternative religion. But more on that later.

So, not everyone was in agreement in AD325. We could say that the Council of Nicaea closed the door on the Messianic Jewish Church. I can't help but wonder if the Church hadn't distanced itself from its Jewish roots at Nicaea, if it had honoured this aspect of Apostolic teaching, that perhaps the fragmentation story might have been different. But that is just speculation on my part.

Nevertheless, we can consider that Nicaea represented the high watermark of Church unity, as it was the first and, sadly, the last time the whole Church reached an agreement on a doctrinal statement. It was pretty much downhill thereafter as differences magnified, tensions rose, personalities clashed, defensiveness reigned, criticism flowed, the precedency of one patriarchy over others was contested as Kings, Princes and Emperors weighed in. The Church was no longer exclusively a religious entity but increasingly became part of the state apparatus. In a little over a century later the first of the major schisms happened. If you want to know the details on this and the rest of the ecclesiastical fractures that ensued, there are many learned tomes that will educate you on the subject; there is also, the much less learned but also entertaining, Ancient & Modern: The Search.

Looking at the positives of that event however, we can say that **in the Nicene Creed** we may have something that could be used to define the **Core Christian Truths** as passed down **from the Apostles,** albeit with a caveat about the separation from its Judaic roots.

10. Burn the Heretic!

With whom exactly, are we supposed to be in unity? Christians obviously, but which congregations are considered Christian? The only answer to that question has to be who holds to the Core Truths attested to in scripture. As I have presented, we could use the Nicene Creed as a succinct summary but there is another, more fool-proof method.

The Witness of the Holy Spirit

In the book Ancient & Modern: The Search, the heroine on her journey through church history inevitably encounters several pseudo-Christian sects. In writing about these encounters I chose not to have her consult a list of acceptable doctrines with which to inform her position, and to help her decide which side of the truth line these sects were upon. I took it out of the domain of man's (or woman's) clinical decision-making and instead left it to the discernment of the Holy Spirit. **The witness of the Holy Spirit within a Christian is more than capable of alerting us to heresy**, without consulting a definitive list, such as the Nicene Creed. Hence in the book the heroine several times remarks that she, "Just knew they were wrong," without specifically realising that this was the gift of discernment given by the Holy Spirit.

By conventional wisdom this may look a weak position, (which doesn't really matter as the story is fiction) but please bear in mind that in the divine economy, the Holy Spirit is one hundred percent correct, every time. The hard bit is learning to faithfully hear Him and to not let our own prejudices, traditions or human wisdom get in the way.

Jesus told us that,

'If anyone wills to do His will, he shall know concerning the doctrine, whether it is from God or whether I speak on My own authority.'[1]

Clearly stating that if our heart is right before God, we will know whether doctrine is from God or not. He also said that when it comes to false prophets,

'By their fruit you will know them.'[2]

This is a very well-known principle but notice the specifics of what it is saying. By their fruits (i.e. their actions) then you will <u>know</u> them. In other words: look, see, listen, take-in all that you can and in your heart, in your spirit you will, quite simply, <u>know</u>. If you truly believe that the Holy Spirit lives divinely within you, then He is more than qualified to guide you and to *'keep you from falling'.*[3] So perhaps I wasn't too far from the truth by allowing my heroine to, "Just know."

When it comes to the Core Truths there is perhaps an argument to say there is <u>no list</u> by which we are able to (or it is wise for us to) in our humanity hold up against another group of believers in order to decide whether to include or exclude them. Have we been appointed as judge and jury? As we will see shortly, we have been instructed to *'Judge not!'*[4] but instead to operate in a spirit of grace and openness to all. In this environment, non-Christian sects who are not born of the Spirit of God but from the flesh will become, as the Apostle Paul put it *'self-evident.'* [5] At which point we are rightly advised to give them a wide berth.

As confident as I am that the witness of the Holy Spirit is the ideal way to identify heresy, I am also realistic enough to know that in practice such a position will not be acceptable to some

---

[1] John 7 v 17
[2] Matthew 7 v 16
[3] Jude 1 v 24
[4] Matthew 7 v 1
[5] Galatians 5 v 19

Christians. Therefore, I will have to use a definitive list of core beliefs, and if we need to have such a list, it appears that it can only really be based on the Nicene Creed.

Putting the Nicene Creed to the Test

Theory is fine, but if it seems that the Nicene Creed should work as the only man-made document we could use as our plumbline, then I think we should test it out first to see if it really is safe for us to use in practice.

There are twelve major religions that represent 83% of the population of the world. These are Baha'i, Buddhism, Christianity, Confucianism, Hinduism, Islam, Jainism, Judaism, Shinto, Sikhism, Taoism, and Zoroastrianism.[1] All of these, except Christianity, deny the divinity of Christ. So, we can immediately exclude all of these world religions from our need to consider them as part of the One Church. But that is exactly what we would have expected – no surprises. A word of caution though as we do need to tread a little carefully with Judaism. Judaism and Christianity believe in the same God, and Jews remain God's covenant people, but as they do deny the divinity of Christ most Jews are not part of the One Church.

But it does not follow that every congregation that calls itself Christian does indeed hold to these truths. Heresy is a very specific word. Taken from the Greek word for 'choice', a heretic is one who has firstly identified as a Christian but then has chosen to deny one or more of the essential tenets of the Christian faith. You cannot be a heretic if you are not 'masquerading' as a Christian, otherwise you are just following an alternative belief system. There are plenty of pseudo-Christian groups waiting to confuse and mislead us.

---

[1] Major Religions of the World, 2 July 2021, by infoplease.com

Let's starts by looking at which of the mainstream Christian denominations openly accept all of the tenets on the Nicene Creed.

Christian Denominations that accept the Nicene Creed

Anglican,
Armenian*,
Baptist,
Brethren,
Calvinist,
Catholic,
Church of the East*,
Congregational,
Coptic*,
Eastern Orthodox,
Evangelical,
Greek Orthodox,
Lutheran,
Methodist,
Moravian,
Oriental Orthodox*,
Pentecostal,
Presbyterian,
Reformed,
Russian Orthodox.

* Whilst the Nicene Creed was drafted in at the Council held in 325, various revisions were made at the subsequent Councils of Ephesus (AD431) and Chalcedon (AD451) to counter further heretical ideas at that time. It was at these councils that the first major schisms occurred when the Church of the East, the Coptic Church and Oriental Orthodox Church refused to agree to the revised text. It is outside the scope of this book to expand on the reasons for these splits, but in my opinion, they were less to do with specific doctrinal disagreement and more the assumed supremacy of the Bishop of Rome (with the backing of the Roman Emperor) over the Bishop of Alexandria. Please read and make your own judgement. For me, I consider that they all agreed to the Nicene Creed as drafted in AD325.

We cannot deny that the list of denominations that hold to the Nicene Creed still represents a huge spectrum of variety with regard to church practice, but they all believe the same Core Truths that the Church accepted nearly 1700 years ago. Mind you, this hasn't stopped several of them going to war with each other over that period, but that was often more to do with power, control and money than doctrine and belief.

In antiquity, as we have already seen, the Apostolic and Ante-Nicene Fathers took decisive action to excommunicate heretical sects that threatened to influence and divert the mainstream Church. These actions happened before the Nicene Creed was formulated so we will now take a look at those heresies to see if the Nicene Creed would have resulted in the same outcome. This should help build our confidence in using the Nicene Creed as our yardstick and it may shed light on some modern pseudo-Christian groups that retain some of these ancient heretical beliefs.

Gnosticism

As I have already described, the first and most significant threat to the early Church came from the Gnostics. This heresy evolved out of the Platonist belief that the physical world is bad whereas the unseen (spiritual) world is good. The goal therefore, was to separate yourself as much as possible from the corrupt earthly world and to discover the God within yourself. To achieve this you would need to acquire additional, often secretive, knowledge or 'Gnosis'. This philosophy is echoed today in much of the New Age movement with its focus on alternative lifestyles and gaining knowledge through mystical and internal reflection. Had the early Gnostics continued up to Nicaea they would have not agreed with it, neither do members of today's New Age movement, much of which is pagan in origin.

Another modern-day Gnostic threat comes from those Christian groups who have formulated an alternative belief system based on an interpretation of extra Biblical writings. Growing in popularity this movement feeds into and from the so-called Conspiracy Theory movement. A careful inspection of such groups must be made as any group that claims that salvation is unobtainable without this extra knowledge, which only they possess, is clearly gnostic.

The attainment of divinity through special revelation was a hallmark of Gnostic belief. Therefore, we would have to include another major modern group that is firmly rooted in that ideology. Scientology, literally means 'The study of knowing'. They openly state that, "god exists, but as to the form in which he exists, we do not know,"[1] and there are, "gods above other gods, and gods beyond the gods of the universes."[2] We can confidently conclude that this group would not agree with every tenet of the Nicene Creed.

Modalism

A second heresy that threatened to derail the early Church was that which we now call Modalism. This originated from a third century theologian named Sabellius who contended that "Father, Son, and Spirit" were different roles played by the same divine person in different circumstances. Another way of describing it was that God wore masks (like an actor) to allow him to play different parts as needed. This meant that when Jesus walked the earth there was no God in heaven, as He was presenting Himself as a man. Following the day of Pentecost God presents himself as the Holy Spirit. Different 'modes' for different times. This teaching denies the doctrine of the Trinity and hence is non-Nicene. Any modern group that denies the Trinity, therefore, fails the Nicene test. This would therefore preclude, amongst others, the following: Christadelphians, Church of the Blessed Hope, Christian Scientists, Dawn Bible Students, Living Church of God, Assemblies of Yahweh, Israelite Church of God in Jesus Christ, Members Church of God International, Unitarian

---

[1] Scientology: A World Religion, p. 17: What is Scientology, p. 200
[2] Scientology 8-8008, p. 72

Christians, Unitarian Universalist Christians, The Way International, The Church of God International, and the United Church of God.[1]

Arianism

Now let's move to the heresies that sought to deny or undermine the divinity of Christ. There were a number of them in the first three centuries of the Church but perhaps the most well documented, and indeed the one that triggered the Council or Nicaea, was that of Arianism. In short, this taught that God the Son was a created being and hence there was a time when He did not exist. This doctrine gained a wide acceptance pre-Nicaea, and as we have already seen the Nicene Creed itself is framed specifically to refute this. It died out in the years following until being resurrected in the nineteenth century by the Church of Jesus Christ of the Latter-day Saints (Mormons) and The Jehovah's Witnesses. We would therefore have to include both of these on the non-Nicene Creed list for, amongst other things, their denial of the divinity of Christ.

The Unification Church, otherwise termed the Moonies, also fails this test, teaching that "Historically, Jesus the Messiah came in Adam's place to restore mankind. He was not deity...it is a great error to think Jesus was God Himself."[2] And also "The cross has been unable to establish the Kingdom of Heaven on Earth by removing our original sin." [3]

My discussion of these various pseudo-Christian groups is not meant to be exhaustive. There are several better texts that explore their beliefs in more detail so I hope you will allow me this cursory assessment.

---

[1] Halsey, A. (13 October 1988). British Social Trends since 1900: A Guide to the Changing Social Structure of Britain. Palgrave Macmillan UK. p. 518. ISBN 9781349194667.
[2] 'Sun Myung and the Unification Church', James Bjornstad, p. 29,30.
[3] 'Understanding the Cults', Josh McDowell and Don Stewart p. 138

I guess, for most seasoned Christians there have been few surprises in these conclusions. Certainly, they were all pretty much as expected. But there are a couple of groups that don't quite fit the cookie-cutter assessment and deserve a more detailed look.

The Great Disappointment

In the book Ancient & Modern: The Search, the heroine witnesses the aftermath of The Great Disappointment of October 22, 1844. If you are unaware of this nation-changing event, then that is one more reason to either buy the book, spend some time on Wikipedia, or accept the following brief précis.

In mid-nineteenth century New England a preacher by the name of William Miller began to teach that he had computed the exact date of Christ's return: October 22, 1844. With hindsight, it is easy to find such a claim as amusing, but at the time he had garnered a huge following. His meetings were so large they were staged in the biggest tent in North America, with seating for four thousand. When the date passed without incident, tens of thousands of faithful souls were left bereft having sold their belongings in anticipation. Hence it became known as The Great Disappointment.

In the immediate aftermath of this event two religious groups formed, each offering a re-interpretation of Miller's patently inaccurate claims. These were the Jehovah's Witnesses, whose errors we have already covered, and also the Seventh Day Adventists. Again, I am not going to go into the doctrinal position of the Seventh Day Adventists, as others are better qualified to do that than I. But as the criterion I am proposing herein is to use the Nicene Creed as the benchmark, then I would have to admit that despite their inauspicious origins, on paper at least they appear to hold to every tenet of the Creed. For me, the jury is still out, I don't know enough about them, and the witness of what I believe to be the Holy Spirit within me is somewhat disquieted, but whether or not that is affected by historic prejudice I am unsure.

Consequently, I would urge you to do your own research before making any judgement on the Seventh Day Adventists.

The Macion Heresy

The final ancient heresy I want us to consider is that of Marcion, which I touched on previously. This was the belief that the God of the Old Testament was different from the God of the New Testament and hence everything to do with the Church's Jewish origins must be purged. Marcion was excommunicated and his teachings rubbished by Irenaeus as well as several other apologists.

However, despite the unanimous rejection of the Church, and Marcion's death, this particular heresy appeared to stick. What is more, the heresy found its way into the mainstream Church, in what we now call Replacement Theology or Supersessionism. It has become acceptable to believe that the Church has replaced Israel in God's affections and that His *"everlasting covenant"*[1] with Abraham has somehow been reassigned. I grew up under this teaching, and accepted it as truth for over forty years. When reading Old Testament scriptures in my mind when I read 'Israel', I would unconsciously substitute it with 'The Church.' What is more, I assumed this was correct.

In the words of William S. Campbell, reader in Biblical Studies at the University of Wales and Senior Research Fellow, at the University of Potsdam, "The question arises... How much Jewishness is really necessary? That is the question repeatedly raised since the time of Marcion, whose stance appears to mark a crucial boundary in the limitation of Jewish influence in Christianity."[2]

Regardless of our personal opinions, or prevalent teaching, we all need to be aware that in the second century it was

---

[1] Genesis 17 vs 4-8
[2] "Understanding Paul's Conception of the Faithfulness of God to Israel" by William S. Campbell, University of Wales, JJMJS No. 2 (2015): 79--101

unanimously decided that the idea of the Church replacing Israel was heresy. Since then, I think that we, the Church, may have failed to fully deal with Marcion's heresy and embrace the Church's Hebraic root.

11. The Difficult Issues that Divide Us.

We need to finish the thought process we started a couple of chapters ago. To remind you, I was reflecting on a conversation I'd had with a friend who considered that church unity can only be built on knowing where two congregations (and by extrapolation denominations) stand on what he called the Primary, Secondary and Tertiary issues. We have spent some time defining the first of these which I called Core Truths.

Let's, for a moment, skip the secondary issues and consider the tertiary ones. When I asked my friend for a definition, he described it as things that were purely down to personal preference, style or tradition and had little bearing on their beliefs. The examples he quoted were, "The types of songs sung, the type of prayers prayed, etc." Again, at first glance this appears to be safe ground. But let's be careful. Consider the case of the Bishop of Brechin in seventeenth century Scotland. At the time, the use of the Book of Common Prayer was so fiercely divisive that at one point he conducted his services with a pair of loaded pistols on his pulpit, aimed squarely at the congregation, making sure they prayed the right way![1] Prayer was clearly not a tertiary matter to him.

And what if my friend's off-the-cuff examples had included: whether there was a cross in the church building; or whether the communion table was called an altar; or if paintings or statues are considered to be a form of worship; whether the minister wore robes; or if he were to be called father; or countless other seemingly innocuous things. Had some of these been his examples, I may have had to point out that they had all been the cause of not only church division but in some cases bloodshed. Whilst they may be Tertiary issues to some, to others they are (or were) worth fighting for.

---

[1] "Reformation Christianity" by Peter Matheson Fortress Press p86

That being said, I am, of course in agreement that there are a lot of things that differ between congregations and denominations which are a matter of style, preference or even just tradition and aren't a serious point of conflict to either party.

This book is seeking to address how we are meant to behave towards each other when there are serious differences. So, we can't avoid it; we are going to have to consider the more contentious middle ground, what he called the secondary issues.

Secondary Issues

Asking my friend to give me a definition of what constituted a <u>secondary</u> issue was much harder to pin down. It was clear that there were certain beliefs that if a congregation were to hold, he would find it near impossible to have anything to do with them.

Whilst he didn't articulate it as such, I have heard it stated elsewhere that a congregation holding a position that is not deemed to be sound doctrine, would be considered as being 'in error' on that issue. Consequently, to be 'in fellowship' with them would be tantamount to compromise. I perceive that this is a commonly held, although rarely verbalised, stance across the Church as we are much too polite.

This stance might just be at odds with Jesus' command to demonstrably act in love towards every other part of the One Church, even if we disagree. Did He not say,

'This is My commandment, that you love one another as I have loved you.' [1]

And how did He love us?

---

[1] John 15 v 12

111

'God demonstrates His own love toward us, in that while we were still sinners, Christ died for us.' [1]

Whilst we were opposed to Him – He acted in love towards us. Not that the love was theoretical or on some conceptual spiritual plane; no, he <u>demonstrated</u> His love toward us – *'Even the death of the cross.'* [2]

Distancing oneself from other parts of the One Church, no matter how pious we consider it to be, is incompatible with the command to exercise brotherly (or sisterly) love.

How do we decide which people, congregations and denominations constitute this One Church? My conviction is that it includes <u>all</u> of those that hold to the Nicene Creed. Using that as the datum we then have to accept that some will hold opposing views on some significant doctrines.

Back in chapter nine of this book I asked you to look at about fifty points of difference between denominations and to decide whether you would consider someone who held the opposing view to yourself as a being Christian or not. In choosing these questions I was, of course, being selective. I deliberately avoided some of the doctrinal and structural issues that have been such a point of disagreement over the years that they were either the seed of major schism or the final straw that sealed it. But now is not the time to shy away from these contentious issues, so if you are ready to explore these so-called secondary issues, lets dive in.

There have always been contentious issues in the Church. Some of the current live issues which jump to mind include the role of women in leadership and the inclusion of people from the LGBT community. A few decades ago, the hot topic was the validity of the gifts of the Holy Spirit (or at least it was in my experience). Wind the clock back a few more decades and the

---

[1] Romans 5 v 8
[2] Philippians 2 v 8

prevalence of the so-called Social Gospel took centre-stage, a few more decades back and you would have found that alcohol, tobacco and gambling had become the flash points. A further few decades back and the Church was wrestling with the issue of slavery which then morphed into the idea of racially separate congregations. Years before, we see the desire to separate the Church from the State led to the establishment of several new denominations. Further back the use of the Bible in the common language, the proscribing of liturgy and the authority of bishops were all fiercely divisive topics.

Continuing back in time, we hit The Reformation of 1517 where the authority of the Church as the only means of salvation is challenged, and within a few years, issues of interpretation between protestant streams surfaced which included the nature of Christ's presence in the Eucharist, predestination and baptism, to name a few. Back in the middle-ages the issues tended to be more political in nature with the assumed superiority of the Church of Rome leading to the Great Schism of 1054. Even further back, we would have found that the divisive issues were more doctrinal as the early Church wrestled with seemingly crazy new ideas such as the Trinity and Christ being both man and God. And throughout the whole of history, you can insert the timeless question of "How should Christianity respond to, or be part of, the culture of the day?" I cover many of these historical examples in the book Ancient & Modern: The Search so forgive me not expanding on the details here.

This list is not exhaustive, but you will see that there have been a lot of very contentious issues over which arguments have been voiced, books written, synods held, tears shed and in too many cases blood spilled. There has scarcely been a time over the last seventeen hundred years when there has not been a subject with which we, His Church, have not fiercely disagreed with ourselves.

I am going to attempt to bring some understanding to this perpetual failing. To do so I will use a few examples from the above list, starting with the theological doctrine we call Predestination.

Predestination

Let me attempt to explain what Predestination is. One side of the debate, the Calvinist position, is that God, who exists outside of time, knew in advance every person who would accept the saving grace of the cross. Hence when Jesus died, He, being God, did so for those whom he already foreknew would accept His salvation. By extension, whilst we appear to have free will, we are nonetheless 'predestined' to be saved as God already knew we would be. The alternative viewpoint, known as Arminianism, is rather simpler to express. Jesus died for everyone, and we all have free will to accept it or not. Importantly the Arminian view states that God's saving grace is resistible, whereas the Calvinist position is that it is not. Well, that's my simple definition.

The two opposing factions faced-off against each other at the Synod of Dort (1618) barely one hundred years after the Protestant Reformation. The Synod was a bruising affair, with the Calvinists in the ascendancy trouncing the Arminians through sheer weight of numbers. There was little grace exhibited at Dort and its outcome was the establishment of two opposing streams of the Protestant Church that continue to this day as well as the initiation of different translations of the Bible. Again, I am not going to spend too long going over the history, nor proffer my own view. Rather and most importantly I want to focus on the outcome. I don't mean the immediate aftermath – more the long-term legacy.

There are literally thousands of denominations whose official position falls either side of the Calvinist-Arminian divide. In order to help you, I will attempt to summaries which key 'brands' exist on each side.

Forgive me using the term 'brands' for the description of a denomination but it is exactly the right term to use. Imagine, for example, you were on holiday, or on a business trip, in say Central America and wanted to go to church but didn't know which church to go to and had no one to ask. If you pulled up outside the National Evangelical Presbyterian Church of Guatemala the word that you would latch on to would be Presbyterian which ought to convey something of its ethos. Just like a consumer brand is carefully crafted to convey a message or an idea, that is over and above the product itself, which will assure the consumer of what the product will be like before they buy it. In a similar way the word 'Presbyterian' acts as a brand to enable you, the church consumer, to quickly assess its identity, doctrine, style, before you commit to step inside. I guess you might also focus on the word Guatemala, and decide if your Spanish was likely to be good enough, before entering!

That being said, I have used 'brands' in my attempt to formulate a table to explain what the Calvinist-Arminian divide looks like today.

Calvinist	Arminian
Thousands of denominations, often with **Calvinist, Reformed, Congregational** or **Presbyterian** in their description.	Thousands of denominations including the original **Methodists, Baptists**, and **Salvation Army**.
Also, we can include the **Church of Scotland**	We can include most **Evangelical, Pentecostal** and **Charismatic** churches
Both / Neither	
The **Anglican** Church The **Lutheran** church	

I had expected this to be a reasonably simple exercise, but to my surprise I found that on investigation most of the denominations now have a more relaxed stance on the subject of predestination. Most are at pains to stress they are more than willing to accept people from 'the other side!'

How curious? What was fiercely contested in 1618, now does not appear to be quite so important. Is it just time that has softened the protagonists' views? Or has it been a recognition that the millions of Christians on either side of the debate have been used by God in magnificent and dramatic ways regardless of their opinion on this particular doctrine. Were the differences in belief on this seemingly vitally important matter really that... important?

Let's consider a real example from history. Many will be aware of the origins of the Methodist movement whose founders were not only John & Charles Wesley but also the great preacher George Whitefield. Whitefield later moved to North America and became one of the major players in the outpouring in the early eighteenth century which became known as the Great Awakening. This was where the term 'revival' was first used. Whitefield and John Wesley preached the gospel of Christ, and through their ministry and God's grace, tens of thousands were saved. However, George Whitefield was an ardent Calvinist whereas John Wesley was a determined Arminian. At length, they would debate these mutually exclusive positions, neither giving ground.

There is evidence to suggest that this is where the expression "Agree to disagree" was first used. Certainly, that is the philosophy they adopted between themselves. They decided that their beliefs about predestination were not as important an issue in the eighteenth century as they had been at Dort in 1618. Interestingly, and most importantly, neither of them ever felt the need to change their views. We can learn a lot from the fact that **having a fundamental difference didn't prevent them working together** for the sake of the gospel.

,   Let's leave predestination and move onto the equally thorny issue of transubstantiation.

Transubstantiation

I am going to use the term Transubstantiation (used in the Catholic Church) as shorthand to also include the terms 'Consubstantiation' (used in The Lutheran Church), 'Trans-elementation' (used in The Eastern Orthodox Churches) or simply 'Change' (used in The Oriental Orthodox & Coptic Churches). The precise details differ slightly between denominations but in short it is the belief that during the Eucharist the sacramental bread and wine transform into the body and blood of Christ (or at least they coexist with Him at that moment). The opposing view is that these elements are merely symbolic.

To help understand how symbols can take on a more important meaning let me offer an oversimplistic example. For some, wearing a wedding ring is merely a symbol of their marital status but for others it is more. In a strange way it allows the wearer to consider their spouse to be ever-present with them. Not a brilliant example but you get the idea.

In the days after the Protestant Reformation it became a hugely divisive issue. In 1529 the leaders of the two simultaneous reformations, the German Martin Luther and the Swiss Ulrich Zwingli, attempted to unite their opposing positions on several subjects, including transubstantiation. They literally sat across the table from each other at Marburg Castle and, having reached agreement on many, many subjects, it was transubstantiation that would prove to be a bridge too far. The debate got so heated that Luther famously chalked onto the wooden table top the Latin phrase: 'Hoc est corpus meum' or 'This is my Body', to make his point. Luther was of the belief that if Jesus said it was His body, then it must be His body and not merely a symbol. To believe anything else would be to call Jesus a liar. Zwingli disagreed and considered the doctrine to be somewhat akin to believing in magic. The meeting broke down with both parties entrenched in their positions and the outcome of the Marburg Colloquy was the failure to unite the Calvinist and Lutheran reformations. The official position of the Lutheran Church, the Catholic Church and all forms of Orthodoxy all hold to the doctrine of transubstantiation. Given the numerical weight of the combined Catholic and Orthodox traditions it would appear that most Christian are of this belief.

Now let's consider these opposing positions, objectively.

Firstly, it is important to understand that for those who hold to Luther's position, the change in the Eucharistic elements is believed to be 'in substance' or 'in essence' and not a change 'in appearance' which of course would become self-evident by taste or visual inspection. The importance of this change therefore is that it allows the 'real presence of Christ' to be at the Eucharist, allowing the communicant to participate in a spiritual encounter with the risen Christ. Thus, it is important that the sacramental elements are elevated to more than mere symbols, they are something sacred, something holy.

When it comes to holy symbols it is pointed out that there is a precedent set in the Old Testament within the holy tabernacle and temple. Whilst one could accurately describe the Ark of the Covenant as a man-made, gold-gilded acacia wooden box, we know that as it contained the very presence of almighty God its holiness made it transcend from merely a box to something far more sacred.

If you were to ask any church that holds the opposite, Zwingli, belief whether they consider the Eucharist service to be sacred or holy, how do you think they would answer? I suspect that if you asked that question to a thousand churches, you would struggle to find a single one who said they did not consider it to be a most sacred practice. I suspect you would find that they hold it at a specially designated time, in a special place, with a special liturgy, administered by an appointed person, using special plates, cups and tablecloths. In short, they hold the Eucharistic meal in great reverence.

Whilst it was Zwingli that led the entrenched position against Luther in 1529, it was John Calvin who, a little while later, documented the doctrinal position of what we now term the Calvinist tradition. In describing the Eucharist he affirmed that what actually happens, 'was a mystery. It could be that the Holy Spirit raises up the church to fellowship with Christ or that the Holy Spirit causes Christ to descend to commune with the church. In either case, there is a spiritual presence of Jesus Christ which goes beyond just mere memorial.' [1]

Personally, I'm not seeing a huge difference in these two opposing positions. Don't misunderstand me, I personally fall on one side of the divide, but to me the divide isn't that clearly defined as it must have appeared to have been across the table at Marburg Castle.

Maybe I am not the only one. A survey in February 2019 by the Pew Research Centre amongst American Catholics found that seven-in-ten (69%) said that they personally believed that during the Catholic Mass, the bread and wine used in Communion "Are symbols of the body and blood of Jesus Christ."[2] That is, despite the official Catholic position, over two-thirds of the members consider them to be no more than symbols. What is even more surprising was that nearly two-thirds of those people believe that their church teaches that they are symbols. If that is what they believe, perhaps on a local level that is what is being taught.

---

[1] 'Historical Theology: An Introduction to Christian Doctrine' by Gregg Allison Zondervan Academic. Quoted in 'Transubstantiation, Consubstantiation, or Something Else? Roman Catholic vs. Protestant Views of the Lord's Supper' October 20, 2017 zondervanacademic.com
[2] 'Just one-third of U.S. Catholics agree with their church that Eucharist is body, blood of Christ' by Gregory A. Smith, 5 August 2019 extracted from www.pewresearch.org

Both sides of this previously fiercely contested, and somewhat intransigent issue, now consider the Eucharist to be sacred and a time where the participants are able to meet with Christ in a spiritual way. Perhaps I am being over simplistic but objectively, with the passage of time, can we really now consider either side to be that different from the other? And yet we have a major fissure in the Church emanating from what was at the time, a so-called secondary issue. It certainly wasn't a primary one as neither side considered the other to be heretical, nor was it a tertiary one as the division was actual and long-lasting.

For another example of a secondary issue that caused a significant divide, we could look at the issue of Slavery. In the book Ancient & Modern: The Search I go into a detailed comparison of the arguments that were used at the time both for and against slavery. I specifically chose this issue as a worked example of how the Bible can be used by either side of an argument to perfectly defend their position. In the book, on listening to the well-defended arguments of each side, our heroine finds herself unsure of what she believed on the subject. I'm not going to repeat the discourse here (one more reason to read the book) suffice it to say that the Bible is a powerful weapon; the danger comes when it is used by both sides of an argument.

Acceptance

Predestination, transubstantiation, slavery as well as many other topics have, in their time, been hugely divisive issues; neither side being willing to compromise and both able to passionately and convincingly defend their positions from the Bible. Earlier, when we were thinking about differences of style or practice, I did make the point that even some of these, in previous centuries, had also been the cause of conflict.

However, and this is the really important point, these subjects appear to be less 'charged' now than they were at the time. It looks like the issues which caused division within the Church then are no longer the divisive issues now. What was a secondary issue, has now become no more than a tertiary issue. If this is true, then that's quite profound.

Considering church history, it appears to me that the tangible difference between a secondary and a tertiary issue has principally been the passage of time. Initially, a fiercely defended subject that was divisive, years later (often centuries later) may remain a point of difference but is no longer a cause for debate or conflict.

This looks like a very positive outcome – in essence, Wesley and Whitefield's 'Agree to disagree' principle – where one part of the Church can deliberately <u>accept</u> the beliefs and practices of another, so long as it doesn't mean it has to <u>agree</u> with it. For example:

> "You may use a written liturgy... but I won't,"
> "You may speak in tongues... but I won't,"
> "You may use a modern Bible translation... but I won't,"
> "You may honour icons and statues... but I won't,"
> "You may be led by the Pope... but I'm not,"
> "You may use guitars in church... but I won't,"
> "You may celebrate Saint's days... but I don't."
> And so forth.

How can this mellowing have happened? Some of these subjects were so irreconcilably divisive that at the time there was zero chance of accepting that the alternative interpretation was valid. Can we really conclude that the divisive issues of yesterday will become the noted differences, the minor issues of today? If it is true then we must consider what has happened over the intervening years. With the passage of time (and the passing of the main protagonists) I perceive that:

- There is the self-evident realisation that God uses those who hold alternative views. As God's work increases people are changed and there is growth,

... leading to

- Humble acknowledgement that there may well be more than one interpretation on a given subject,

... opening the door to

- Accepting the validity of those who hold alternative views, and accepting them in love, without resorting to the drawing of swords or poisoned pens.

And if this can be achieved with neither side changing nor compromising their own views, then it truly is a powerful learning point that can help us. In short, the transition from a divisive issue to one that is less so, appears to be a matter of **humble and loving recognition that Christians may hold different views, not a matter of personal doctrinal compromise.**

Also, let's be brutally honest with ourselves. It may not just be the passage of time that allows acceptance. It is likely that the Church simply treads clumsily across the minefield of schism, igniting explosive issue after explosive issue – each successive generation is forced into refocusing the discordant debate. The wounds from the previous fight now become less important in the light of fresh bruises. Perhaps I am being a little harsh, but it does appear that we've bounced from one divisive issue to the next for centuries.

Current Divisive Issues

What are today's bruises? None of the subjects I have discussed so far in this chapter were the examples of Secondary Issues that my friend gave me. His were much more current, much more contentious. So, put your tin hat on again and we'll continue. When I pressed him for subjects that could potentially drive a wedge between himself and any congregation that believes or practises them, he gave me two examples. Firstly,

"The role of women in church leadership," and secondly,

"How the LGBT community should be included and/or accepted within the church."

For the sake of neutrality let me outline the debate. Some people believe that women should not be in a position of leadership in the Church. Whilst this is neither culturally nor politically correct it is nonetheless readily defendable Biblically and consequently one which many major denominations have wrestled with over the last few decades. The opposing view is simply that women can, dependent upon gifting, hold equal roles to men. There are several other compromise positions, spanning the middle-ground between these poles. This is the ecclesiastical battleground upon which much spiritual blood has already been spilled in the debating chamber.

Regarding the topic of sexuality, again, this is a subject causing profound soul-searching within all churches as they consider what their stance should be. At one end are those who believe all forms of homosexuality to be carnal sin; at the other end are those teaching non-judgemental acceptance of the individuals involved. One is focused on the act, the other the person and, of course, there are all stops in between.

As already stated, it is outside the scope of this book for me to share my personal opinions (or those held by my friend) on these issues, which would only serve to position myself as being either on your side or not. At which point you would probably close the book and miss out on all the good stuff yet to come! I do note, however, that in naming these two subjects my friend picked two divisive and particularly painful topics.

Let us look back for a moment at the point I made a few paragraphs earlier. I postulated that: The divisive issues of yesterday will become the accepted points of difference for today. Well, now I have opened these two ultra-hot topics, I can already hear the voices...

"That may have been digestible in the context of historical obscure doctrines, but to consider that today's divisive issues, especially these, will somehow abate over time... well that is at best wishful thinking but probably more akin to a compromise too far!"

Don't worry, my tin hat is securely in place. I know that these two examples will cause many to recoil at the very idea of ever coming into agreement with someone on the other side. And bizarrely I feel the same. But this isn't about compromise or even changing your opinions. Remember, we have seen that Luther, Zwingli, Calvin, Wesley, Whitefield, and others all kept hold of their personal beliefs despite the venom being released at the time. If you were alive a few centuries ago you would have been equally zealous about subjects which from our point of view now appear to be less important, or even somewhat trivial. Did you know, for example, that the seemingly innocuous phrase "The Holy Spirit proceeds from The Father and The Son" caused a lot of trouble. It was this phrase that resulted in people being killed and was the reason the Church was irreconcilably split between Catholic and Orthodox in 1054.[1] But now... is it really an issue at all?

Please embrace the passion you have on these difficult live painful subjects, it is part of what makes you, you. It is part of what God has sown into you. No one is asking you to compromise your firmly held beliefs. But there is a bigger picture and we will get to that in a few chapters' time.

There are No Secondary Issues

For now, let me just say it as I now see it. Based on what we have seen in history, I suggest that there is no difference between what we were calling secondary and tertiary issues other

---

[1] The filioque controversy stemmed from the Roman church unilaterally adding the phrase 'and the son' (Latin 'Filioque) to the Nicene Creed which ultimately led to the East-West Schism of 1054

than the degree of zeal by which each party seeks to defend them. Don't misunderstand me, I acknowledge the feelings of incompatibility with which these issues present; my point is that such feelings applied to <u>all</u> such past differences not just the current <u>live</u> and contentious ones.

If I am correct in this supposition, then we need <u>only</u> consider the primary issues, the <u>Core</u> <u>Truths</u>. Everything else falls into the same basket, requiring grace and acceptance.

One of the greatest theologians that the Church has ever known, Augustine of Hippo (354-430), was of the same opinion. His famous and oft-quoted credo was:

"In essentials, unity; in non-essentials, liberty; in all things, charity,"

If I may paraphrase the great man, he states, 'There are only Core Truths – everything else, no matter how divisive, requires liberty and charity on our part.

This therefore raises a huge behavioural problem for us. How do we relate to a Christian, or for that matter a congregation or denomination, that believes something with which we are violently and passionately opposed? That is the whole point of this book and once we crack this then, and only then, will real demonstrable unity ever be possible.

Read on, dear reader, read on. You're doing fine.

Challenge 3: Acting with Demonstrable Unity

12. Disputes over Doubtful Things.

Black and White

We Christians do have a tendency to paint things in stark black or white. An issue is either right or wrong, either good or bad and there is pretty much nothing in-between. There is zero room for any wishy-washy shade of grey, because that would smack of that most terrible of taboos – compromise.

I read an interesting article recently by Christian author Jonathan Malm, who said, "Christians don't have to bathe the world in black and white. God paints with a canvas of infinitely glorious colours – more colours than our eyes can perceive. Shouldn't we paint with those same colours? My job as a believer is not to project black and white onto others... As it says in Matthew 5:13-16, my job is simply to be salt and light. I'm supposed to bring out the God-flavours and God-colours in this world. Salt doesn't create flavour. It opens the taste buds to receive it. Light doesn't create colour. It simply reveals it." [1]

I love the analogy. God paints in many different colours and so should we. What does that mean for us in practice, in a Church landscape that can appear to be devoid of any form of nuance.

But at times I think we have such a pathological aversion to anything lukewarm that our default position tends to be a declaration of "No compromise" as the tins of Midnight Black and Titanium White are opened.

That there are many subjects upon which Christians disagree is quite an understatement. Whether these are the

---

[1] "You Shouldn't Have an Opinion On Everything" by Jonathan Malm, 30 Aug 2017. www.relevantmagazine.com

ancient doctrinal disagreements that fractured the early Church; or the matters of governance that spawned schisms over the following thousand years; or the diversity of interpretations that was the biproduct of the Protestant Reformation; or the polarising attempts to navigate our modern-day cultural minefield. Whatever the issue – you can probably find different parts of the Church that hold opposing views.

Biblical Ambiguity

Each side of these debates, of course, can claim to be the holder of the genuine Biblical truth of the subject. So how can it be possible for two sides of a disagreement to both anchor their positions in the same source material? Any dispassionate observer looking at Christianity might well ask, "Wouldn't it have been better if the Bible was less ambiguous on some subjects, so they would all believe the same thing?" A logical question but let me offer you an alternative viewpoint.

We know that the Bible can and has been used to defend opposite viewpoints. We also know that God is sovereign, His word is infallible, and He makes no mistakes. Is it not therefore plausible that God, in His infinite wisdom, has <u>allowed</u> such potential ambiguity to exist. Why would He? The answer to me is clear – because unity trumps uniformity. In the full knowledge that there would be subjects upon which we would never reach a consensus, maybe God has set us the task of **sorting things out between ourselves**. After all, is not learning to relate together, to resolve conflict, and to act in demonstrable unity despite our disagreements, the ultimate demonstration of our *'love one for another.'* [1]

If it is true that God has <u>deliberately</u> left room for us to disagree, then it changes the whole dynamic.

---

[1] John 13 v 35

128

What if all the difficult issues that confronted the Church over the last two millennia were precisely the opportunities God gave us to demonstrate that we have His heart for each other. Maybe, over the centuries, He has presented His Church with canvas after difficult canvas precisely in order to teach us how to paint with His colours – not with the feared grey of compromise, but with His vivid hues of love, grace and acceptance.

Disputes over Doubtful Things

If this is true, then we would expect to find in scripture very clear instruction on how to deal with such difficult issues and voila! there it is in Romans 14. Here Paul gives the clearest explanation of how disagreements should be handled. It deals specifically with the dispute that arises when two people, or groups of people, or congregations or denominations, disagree, or as he succinctly puts it, *'Disputes over doubtful things.'*[1]

What does he mean by doubtful things? These are subjects that are not crucial to salvation, not the Core Truths as we put it earlier. And, as we have seen, that basically means everything else. Not to put too fine a point on it, you can probably find disagreement within the Church on literally everything else.

In Romans 14 Paul focuses on two subjects that were clearly the hot topics of that day, but ones that today we might feel quite dispassionate about. First is the issue of what it is permissible for a Christian to eat.

'For one believes he may eat all things, but he who is weak eats only vegetables. Let not him who eats despise him who does not eat, and let not him who does not eat judge him who eats; for God has received him.' [2]

Paul addressed this issue a year earlier in his letter to the church in Corinth at which time he was more specific in saying that

---

[1] Romans 14 v 1
[2] Romans 14 vs 2-3

it was about whether a Christian should eat meat that had been sacrificed to idols.[1] The second issue concerned whether certain days should be observed as more holy than others.

'One person esteems one day above another; another esteems every day alike. Let each be fully convinced in his own mind. He who observes the day, observes it to the Lord; and he who does not observe the day, to the Lord he does not observe it.'[2]

As this epistle is addressed to the church in Rome – a church set up within a large Jewish enclave within a populous gentile city – we are probably safe to assume that the contentious holy days are likely to be the Biblical feasts of Passover, Pentecost and Tabernacles.

Now please note this very important fact. At no point does Paul state on which side of these disputes he personally stands, which he could easily have done. We know from history that Paul celebrated the Biblical feasts, as did all of the Apostles and most of the early church fathers. But this chapter isn't about holy days observance nor dietary rules, it is about dealing with disagreement.

So, let's look at how the scriptures help us with guidance on how to do this. Paul's opening remark is an unequivocal statement that we should not pass judgement upon each other.

'Who are you to judge another's servant? To his own master he stands or falls. Indeed, he will be made to stand, for God is able to make him stand.'[3]

We are all servants of The Most High and answerable to Him alone. Who are we to judge? To leave us in no doubt he then expands the point.

---

[1] 1 Corinthians 8 vs 1-13
[2] Romans 14 vs 5-6a
[3] Romans 14 v 4

'Why do you judge your brother? Or why do you show contempt for your brother? For we shall all stand before the judgment seat of Christ. For it is written:
"As I live, says the LORD,
Every knee shall bow to Me,
And every tongue shall confess to God."
So then, each of us shall give account of himself to God.' [1]

There at the end we have the key point. We each will have to give an account of ourselves; not give an account of others, nor an account as to why we consider that we are right, and others are… less right.

Is it just a male thing or is it just part of our fleshly nature to compare ourselves with others to make ourselves feel better? Perhaps that is just me? This aspect of our flesh needs to be put to death in Christ. When Paul likened Christians to athletes, he didn't mean that we were competing against each other – this is not an inter-church race.

Judge Not?

In starting Romans 14 by emphasising the foundational importance of not judging each other, Paul is echoing the Sermon on the Mount where Jesus stated, again unambiguously, *'Judge Not'* [2]

This is a clear and explicit command from both Paul and Jesus – we are not supposed to judge other people. There appears to be little margin for ambiguity. This is especially true if we understand what is really meant by the word 'judge'.

The words used by Jesus and Paul and translated as judge, whilst not being identical, both come from the Greek verb Krino – to separate, to decide, to judge. Krino is a verb with no fewer than 40 derivations used in the New Testament which are translated

---

[1] Romans 14 vs 7 - 12
[2] Matthew 7 v 1

into a wide spectrum of words including: conclude, condemn, consider, decide, determine, discern, evaluate, go to law, judge, pass judgment, pronounce, regard, stand trial, sue and weigh carefully. The understanding of the nuances of this Greek verb is frankly beyond me so I turned for help to Thayer's Greek Lexicon. Thayer categorises the various uses of the verb Krino into seven broad meanings:

1 - to separate, put asunder; to pick out, select, to choose
2 - to approve, esteem, to prefer
3 - to be of opinion, to deem, to think
4 - to determine, to resolve, to decree
5a – to judge, to pronounce an opinion concerning right and wrong
5b – to judge, to pronounce judgement upon, to subject to censure, to condemn
6 - to rule, to govern; to preside over with the power of giving judicial decisions
7 - to contend together, to dispute, to go to law, to have a suit at law

It is self-evident that there is a wide diversity of meanings represented here. For example, I may prefer Cadbury chocolate to Hershey's, but I am not empowered to pass a judicial decision on the matter. With such a diversity in meaning, which of these uses correlates to the verb forms used by Jesus in Matthew 7 and Paul in Romans 14? According to Thayer they both align with meaning 5b – to judge, to pronounce judgement upon, to subject to censure, to condemn.

That puts a whole new meaning on '*Judge Not.*' Jesus isn't saying don't think, don't choose, don't prefer, don't have an opinion. He is simply saying don't pronounce judgement upon, do not condemn. The clear implication being that you do not have the authority to condemn; this being explicitly stated, as we have seen, by Paul in Romans 14 v 4. Perhaps 'Judge Not' would have been better translated as 'Condemn Not, that you be not Condemned,' but I am not a Bible translator.

We know that someone who pronounces judgement upon someone, or something is called, hardly surprisingly, a judge. A judge is appointed to decide between a variety of outcomes. They may be appointed to decide the guilty party in a court case, or to judge a sporting contest; or the acts in a talent show; or the best in breed at an agricultural fair; or the best cake at the village fete; as well as dozens of other scenarios. In every case there are two essential features that characterise someone as being a judge.

The first of them is that they must be impartial. It stands to reason that you cannot faithfully judge anything unless you are neutral and have no vested interest. Anyone acting as a professional sports umpire or referee who favoured one team over the other would quickly be exposed and duly dismissed. Judging requires impartiality.

But just as importantly, judging requires expertise. A judge must be an expert on the subject they are judging otherwise they are just giving an uninformed personal opinion. There is no point in asking me to choose which prize bull was the best at the county fair. All I know about bulls is that they are best avoided. Being asked to judge cakes, however, that would be much more enjoyable. But as I have only ever baked one cake, a Swiss roll which didn't roll (more of a Swiss fold in reality) I'm the least qualified to judge cakes. All I would give would be my preference, not an expert judgement, on which was best. The only way that anyone can pass a truthful judgement on anything is from the position of both impartiality and expertise.

When it comes to judging our fellow believers only God is qualified.

'You shall not show partiality in judgment... for the judgment is God's.' [1]

---

[1] Deuteronomy 1 v 17

So, not only are we commanded to not judge (i.e. condemn) each other, we are also patently unqualified to do so.

That point made, let's now look at the practical help that Paul gives us in Romans 14 to understand how we are supposed to behave when disagreement surfaces, which I have laid out as a series of behavioural principles.

Principle 1: If you're okay with something, don't look down on those who aren't (or vice versa).

In saying that, *'One believes he may eat all things, but he who is weak eats only vegetables,'* [1] it would be easy to infer that strong Christians have liberty whereas weak Christians have self-imposed constraints. But that is not the point of this passage. Paul goes on to say that the strong should bear with the weak and not try to force them to change. That is the sign of a strong Christian.

'We then who are strong ought to bear with the scruples of the weak, and not to please ourselves. Let each of us please his neighbour for his good, leading to edification. For even Christ did not please Himself.' [2]

Besides, a person who criticises will <u>always</u> think of themselves as the strong one on any particular issue – even if they aren't.

Principle 2: Don't lay down stumbling blocks for others.

Paul then goes further than just considering how we think about a Christian who believes or does something we disagree with. Changing our thoughts is the first step, but we also need to act in love towards them. Love reaches out. Love takes action and, in this context, we are instructed to make sure that our views do not prompt us into putting a stumbling block in their way.

---

[1] Romans 14 v 2
[2] Romans 15 vs 1 – 3

'Therefore, let us not judge one another anymore, but rather resolve this, not to put a stumbling block or a cause to fall in our brother's way' [1]

This is totally counter intuitive. In the natural our instinct might be to undermine an opponent's argument, but God makes it clear that a Christian with whom we may disagree is not our opponent. More than that, we have a responsibility to look after them and care about their feelings and not to allow this 'doubtful issue' to be a 'stumbling block' to them. This will most likely mean that we will need to look at our own actions and take them in hand for the sake of the sensibilities of our brothers or sisters.

'It is good neither to eat meat nor drink wine nor do anything by which your brother stumbles or is offended or is made weak.' [2]

Notice, it is good to restrain our behaviour specifically to help our brother (or sister) who has different views to ours. This is moving in the opposite spirit to the world.

Principle 3: Be gracious.

As we have seen, differences between believers on core Christian truths is probably a sign that one party has strayed a little into heresy. However, differing on anything else is not so simplistic. In the fiery heat of a disagreement we may consider a subject to be an absolutely black and white issue. However, we should really start with the assumption that all things (outside of core truth) may be painted with other colours.

In these areas of difference, both sides should seek to honour God in their own way. If we allow it to deteriorate into arguments then we forfeit any right to say we are honouring God regardless of our position on the issue.

---

[1] Romans 14 v 13

[2] Romans 14 v 21

'Yet if your brother is grieved because of your food, you are no longer walking in love. Do not destroy with your food the one for whom Christ died.' [1]

But what of the knotty question: "If you believe something different to me how can I fellowship with you?"

The first thing to point out is that we are assuming that on this particular issue one party is 'right' and the other party is 'wrong'. It may be the case that in God's economy both sides are operating in His will. Who are we to limit God? If you need an example, consider the Calvinist – Arminian discord we looked at earlier, where both sides of that argument have been used by God mightily over the centuries even though they failed to agree. Our human minds are limited by our own understanding, and we can sometimes see things from a one-dimensional view.

Secondly, whilst we may be sure in our own mind that our position on a difficult issue is sound, and that before God, hand on heart, our conscience is clear, all we are actually deciding is that our position is **right for us.** To extrapolate that into saying that our position is the absolute right one is probably a step too far.

There is often more going on and deeper depths than our mortal minds can comprehend. Consider the example of when Jesus healed a man on the Sabbath, an action which caused some people to be angry with Him for doing so on the holy day. Now those who murmured against him were applying the law of Moses, as they saw it, correctly. In their eyes they were 'right.' Before God they were right, their conscience was clear; and they could no doubt back it up from scripture. But (and it is an important but) they had encountered Jesus who wanted to teach them more than their current understanding. He wanted to open their eyes. As He tried to raise their viewpoint to help them see the bigger picture His response was to say, *'Do not judge by appearance.'* [2]

---

[1] Romans 14 v 15
[2] John 7 v 24

In this example we see that the flashpoint, healing on the Sabbath, was more than a simple right/wrong issue. The same may well be true of any of the difficult subjects upon which we may disagree today.

We read in the Old Testament prophet Isaiah that Jesus never viewed people based on what He sees and hears.

'He shall not judge by the sight of His eyes, nor decide by the hearing of His ears.'[1]

He knew there was more to every person and to every situation. We need to be the same.

So, can we fellowship with those with whom we disagree? Not only can we – we are instructed to. We <u>must</u> be gracious to those that hold different positions. Grace is the <u>only</u> right result.

'Therefore, let us pursue the things which make for peace and the things by which one may edify another.'[2]

Principle 4: Don't be a hypocrite.

On difficult subjects we should attempt to be one hundred percent convinced before God of your own position. But also, remain humble and open-minded to allow the Holy Spirt to steer us. We have seen that it shouldn't be our goal to get as many others as possible to agree with our position. But, sitting on the fence, being double-minded or unsure is an equally dangerous place to be.

'But he who doubts is condemned if he eats, because he does not eat from faith; for whatever is not from faith is sin.'[3]

---

[1] Isaiah 11 v 3
[2] Romans 14 v 19
[3] Romans 14 v 23

It is okay to hold to our personal God-given convictions – they define us. Our actions however need to reflect what we believe while at the same time behaving graciously towards others. This is a balancing act, and we won't always get it right. There is an interesting passage we read in the Epistle to the Galatians where Paul rebuked Peter for acting one way with one group of believers but then changing to acting another way with a different group.[1] Paul openly calls Peter out for hypocrisy. How did Peter get it so wrong? We read in verse 12 that Peter's motivation was fear, not love.

<u>Principle 5: Don't think you have to change your mind but be watchful over yourself.</u>

Amongst all this grace and love-inspired action, no one is saying that you need to change your mind. Obviously, you can change your mind – let's not be intransigent for the sake of pride, but if you are fully sure of your position, no one is saying you need to change it.

'Let each be fully convinced in his own mind.' [2]

Indeed, we should be prepared to explain our position to anyone who asks. Remember, Wesley and Whitefield debated long and hard – but stayed great friends. If appropriate, don't hold back from giving an ardent defence of your position if it's needed.

'Do not let your good be spoken of as evil; for the kingdom of God is not eating and drinking, but righteousness and peace and joy in the Holy Spirit.' [3]

Be sure of your convictions but be humble enough to allow God to guide you – we may get it a little bit wrong sometimes.

---

[1] Galatians 2 vs 11 -14
[2] Romans 14 v 5
[3] Romans 14 vs 16 - 17

'Happy is he who does not condemn himself in what he approves.'[1] and *'Do not use liberty as an opportunity for the flesh.'*[2]

These five principles are there to guide us every time there is a dispute over a doubtful thing. We need to learn how to exercise them.

Preference vs Condemnation

Sadly though, if we look back over the centuries of church history it is easy to see that there has been a lot of judging, a lot of right vs wrong opinions voiced, a lot of condemnation. The result of this disobedience (let's not pretend it is anything else) has inevitably been schism.

Consider though that maybe, throughout all this time, God has been waiting for the day when a disputable topic surfaced, and his Church dealt with it Biblically. By that I mean they take to heart the principles of love and grace He laid out for us, rather than taking and defending polarised positions.

To do so would not diminish anyone's strongly held conviction as there is a big difference between having an opinion or expressing a preference and passing judgement. Let me outline the two alternatives.

One examines something (perhaps a denomination, a congregation, a person, a word, or deed) and compares it with their personal values and beliefs to reach a conclusion. That conclusion can only be something such as: **I like, I dislike, I agree, I disagree, I think it is right, I think it is wrong** and so forth. Not only is this human nature, but it is also entirely acceptable within the Church.

---

[1] Romans 14 v 22
[2] Galatians 5 v 13

The other examines something (a denomination, a congregation, a person, a word or deed) and compares it against an absolute measure to reach a conclusion such as: **It is right or, it is wrong**. The only time this is valid would be in regard to the criteria that we covered in chapter 7 (to decide if something is Christian or not) otherwise this action is never acceptable.

Also bear in mind that if I was to pass judgement upon something (or someone) and consider them as being wrong, can I ever do so impartially? Probably not. If I was impartial then statistically at least, half of the time I would find that I was wrong, and they were right. And what of expertise? To judge, I appoint myself as 'the expert' and the exclusive possessor of truth. This can never be the case. In reality I may simply be no more than the holder of an intransigently held opinion which I may feel the need to defend.

Don't get me wrong, it is okay to have opinions, it is fine to have our own preferences, indeed Paul states that, *'He who is spiritual judges all things.'* [1] But it is not okay to use our preferences as the plumbline by which others are judged. As Jesus said in the Sermon on the Mount (according to my paraphrase): "Do not pronounce judgement, do not condemn."

<u>"I Don't Agree With You."</u>

So where does that leave us? If you haven't already made the connection, some modern-day examples of *'disputes over doubtful things'* are the two examples my friend gave me, which we looked at toward the end of the last chapter. That is permitting women in leadership, and the inclusion of LGBT people fully within the Church. Some congregations, indeed some denominations, are happy to allow women to minister whereas others are not. The same is true for issues of sexuality with some openly accepting those from the LGBT community, whereas others are convinced those choosing to adopt such a lifestyle are being sinful.

---

[1] 1 Corinthians 2 v 15

These are two hotly contested subjects at the moment, but they aren't the only ones. As difficult as it seems, we are instructed not to condemn those on the opposing side of these debates, as being wrong no matter how right we feel we are. But I stress, in not condemning them doesn't make our position on the issue any less the right one <u>for us</u>. It also follows that even if we are 100% convinced of our position it doesn't mean we are 100% correct.

In the heat of contentious disputes there is little use in defending a position Biblically as each would probably be able to do the same. God is not restricted to the dimensions that we are and it is entirely possible that both sides of a debate can represent an aspect of His heart to humanity in a way that we mortals would find it intolerably difficult to do. Such a dichotomy is not evidence that the faith we so passionately follow is somehow vague. On the contrary, it is evidence that we follow an almighty and gracious God who at the same time can be both loving and holy and between these two facets of His character there is no contradiction.

So, how are we to handle ourselves in such debates? Well, wouldn't it be good if we were to use the principles we have just learned and rather than pronouncing judgement, simply stated:

"I don't agree with you – but I may be wrong."

And if someone says that to us, we resist the temptation to get them to agree with us, and lovingly respond with:

"Thank you for listening to my position – I respect yours. I may be wrong too. Now let's have a coffee."

The challenge for us is therefore: **are we sufficiently mature in our faith to allow others to hold views to which we cannot assent, and yet still accept them as our brothers and sisters in the faith**. And I mean accept as equals, not tolerate as being in some way sub-standard, deficient, or lacking the true revelation. Remember, for everyone that we consider to be lacking <u>our</u> revelation, we condemn ourselves to be ignorant of <u>their</u> revelation. Specks and planks in eyes comes to mind.[1]

Notice how in all of his instruction in Romans 14, Paul never says, change your opinion or find a watered-down compromise position that everyone is happy with. I fully expect that in the church in Rome there were two (or maybe more) polarised opinions on these specific disputes. What was miraculous is that it did not result in schism. Why has the Church found it so hard to do the same over the following centuries?

If you'll permit me a simple soundbite to try to emphasise this vitally important point, I will offer the following:

Don't change your convictions – but don't use them to convict others.

Accepting those with an alternative viewpoint on a serious matter can raise questions of how we are to behave towards each other. We will come to that in the next chapter but before we get there, please don't move on until you have got the core of this chapter in your heart. It is that important. I would go as far as to say that if we don't learn this lesson – the One Church <u>cannot</u> be united.

---

[1] Matthew 7 v 5

13. Celebrating Our Uniqueness

God is Pro-individual.

God has fashioned each one of us with unique abilities, talents and gifts and called us into his One Church with a specific purpose and calling. One Church made up of believers across all congregations and all denominations.

But of course, if the Church is a collection of individuals all doing their own thing, it raises the question where is the unity? Where is the common purpose? The answer to this takes us to the glorious understanding that unity is not a result of having a uniform man-made strategy, but through the result of each member finding their own part and submitting to the leadership of the head, Jesus.

There is a genuine unity achievable through submitted individuality, a phenomenon we witness in nature. Perhaps the most beautiful example is the sight of starlings swooping and diving together as they prepare to roost in the autumn evening. This perfectly fluid display, called a murmuration, can involve thousands of birds moving in perfect harmony with each other in a mesmerising aerial dance. They appear to have no leader, no instruction, no rehearsals but, despite this, no two birds collide. They all move in perfect unison.

Members of One Body

God uses several metaphors to describe His multi-individual organisation, but perhaps the most widely used one is to liken it to a body, a human body.

'We who are many are one body'[1] and,

---

[1] 1 Corinthians 10 v 17

'You were called in one body'[1] **and,**
'There is one body'[2] **and,**
'We were all baptized into one body'[3] **and,**
'You are the body of Christ, and members individually'[4] **and,**
'God has set the members, each one of them, in the body just as He pleased.'[5]

I must have preached on this subject dozens of times and I am sure you have heard similar messages over and over again. We are all parts of one body and,

'If the foot should say, "Because I am not a hand, I am not of the body," is it therefore not of the body? And if the ear should say, "Because I am not an eye, I am not of the body," is it therefore not of the body?'[6]

Such a sermon would typically go on to emphasise how every part of the body (i.e. every member of the One Church) is equally important regardless of whether they preach or (insert a typically overlooked role such as serving the teas, doing the flowers or putting out the chairs). It is a very worthy sermon and one which I, and others, have regularly used to emphasise equality of value. We are all equally valuable regardless of what we do or, of course, what we do not do.

'And the eye cannot say to the hand, "I have no need of you"; nor again the head to the feet, "I have no need of you."'[7]

What I had previously failed to realise was that whilst this message is valid, I was missing the whole point. Considering the Church as a body means I must embrace the fact that we are all

---

[1] Colossians 3 v 15
[2] Ephesians 4 v 4
[3] 1 Corinthians 12 v 13
[4] 1 Corinthians 12 v 27
[5] 1 Corinthians 12 v 18
[6] 1 Corinthians 12 vs 15-16
[7] 1 Corinthians 12 v 21

different. This is not just a message of equality of value but one of diversity of <u>function</u>. I guess that is obvious to most, or at least implied, but it is rarely what I've heard taught. Perhaps the next time I preach on the subject I should just stand up and say, "You've got a part to play in the One Church – so get on with it, 'cos no one else is going to do it for you." It may sound a bit harsh, and I'm sure I wouldn't be asked back, but I think the sentiment is right.

If we accept that we are all part of a body, it follows that we are meant to all be different. In fact, you could go as far as saying that the very existence of such differences proves that we are a body.

'For as the body is one and has many members, but all the members of that one body, being many, are one body. But now indeed there are many members, yet one body.' [1]

No two parts of the human body are the same. It's a sweeping generalisation, and probably not entirely accurate on a cellular level, but you get my point. Even the things you have two of – are opposites of each other!

It is almost as though God has designed His One Church to be full of distinct, different, individual, quirky, eccentric, unique and in some cases simply odd people. Why should we be surprised? That is just a reflection of the entire human race which we know God fashioned in His image.[2] What is it that makes us want to impose uniformity across all of this glorious diversity? Might it be a desire to control people? A desire to make others more like... us?

Assuming you are in agreement with this reasoning, and probably castigating me for being slow on the uptake, then come with me as we take a significant mental leap.

---

[1] 1 Corinthians 12 vs 12 & 20
[2] Genesis 1 v 27

Congregational Function

We can readily accept that the body of Christ is made up of many members each with a specific function. Every member of a congregation has a part to play and every one of them is equally valuable. But why stop there? Why only apply this logic within a single congregation? Why not extrapolate the idea to refer to the whole congregation itself and how it fits within the One Church?

Each congregation is both equally <u>valuable</u> and has an essential <u>function</u> to play in the body. This applies whether or not they are part of our denomination, or to speak candidly again, whether or not we share every aspect of their doctrinal interpretation, their organisational structure, their practices or their style.

If that 'other' congregation are genuine believers and the Holy Spirit inside us attests to their inclusion as Christian, then they are part of His body. Each gathering of believers, each congregation and by extension each denomination has its own God-appointed purpose. They have been placed in the body for a specific reason with a specific priority and a specific purpose, at a specific time in a specific place.

For example, I am aware of a congregation in a university city that each year welcomes a high intake of new students, many of which are from church families and for several this is their first time living away from home. This congregation understands what its purpose is and teaches on morality, integrity, faithfulness and Christian service over and over again. There is no point, they consider, on moving too far off this track as the hundreds of lives they impact need to have these solid foundations laid in this formative season of their Christian lives.

Some congregations of my acquaintance give a special emphasis on helping the homeless, or refugees, or running a food bank, or debt counselling. Others I know run a Christian school, or youth club, or work on the streets late at night. One runs an over-

60s' programme, another offers bereavement support, some have services that are in a second language or are signed for the deaf. Other congregations host deep Bible teaching conferences, another provides worship and prophetic events, yet another not only holds prayer meetings but also co-ordinated prayer missions. There are some congregations with healthy relationships with local politicians and businesses, as well as other local influencers. And what is more, all of the examples I have just listed are within a 20-minute drive from my front door. All of these expressions of One Church exist in my locality. Every one of them is valuable and an essential expression of the One Church in my locality. I presume the same will be true for your locality also.

And yet the danger that it is all too easy to resort into is the language of "Come and see what <u>our church</u> is doing." Not only is this sentiment spoken as a kind of badge-of-honour, but at the same time it infers an exclusivity. This is an activity that <u>we</u> are doing, not anyone else. And if you want to get involved then <u>you</u> will have to join <u>our</u> church first. Why is this? Aren't we all part of the same One Church?

Wouldn't it be a much better demonstration of our one-bodyness that within a specific geography each member of every congregation was actively encouraged to participate in the activities that they felt passionate about regardless of whether they were being organised by their own congregation or the one down the road.

'But God composed the body, having given greater honour to that part which lacks it, that there should be no schism in the body, but that the members should have the same care for one another. And if one member suffers, all the members suffer with it; or if one member is honoured, all the members rejoice with it.'[1]

---

[1] 1 Corinthians 12 v 24b - 26

Send Revival

Let me paint a picture for you. Imagine a church in a town, let's call them St. Aiden's (I was going to call it church A, but let's make it more realistic) who are very well-attended and have, amongst other activities, a strong prayer ministry. This prayer ministry has been praying fervently for months and months, for the burden that God has placed upon their hearts. That burden is to pray for revival to come upon their town. So, in faithfulness, in every prayer meeting, house-group, and at every one of their Sunday services for over a year the continual prayer has been, "Lord, send revival."

Unbeknown to them, something amazing has begun to happen at St. Bartholomew's (church B), a little chapel barely a quarter of a mile from their front door, where numbers have begun to swell with people finding faith in Jesus. Already, they cannot accommodate the people flocking to attend their ad-hoc meetings where verifiable healings are being attested to. Their young leader is at pains to try to understand what is going on. All he has done was to faithfully adhere to his church's rites, and yet there is a hunger in the people to a degree he could never have imagined. "Surely, this is revival," he says. Eventually, the leaders of the St. Aiden prayer group hear of the miraculous events happening down the road.

My question to you is as follows, and we are going to have to be honest with ourselves as we consider the answer. In light of what they now know, how would that prayer group at St Aiden's pray? Notice I am saying <u>would</u> pray not <u>should</u> pray – we all know how we should pray. This is a time for honest reflection.

As I see it there are two options:

a) "Hallelujah, thank you God for answering our prayers and sending revival to our town," or

b) "Lord, send revival on us, too."

Lord, forgive us if we ever offer prayer (b) at the expense of prayer (a) ignoring the hundreds of townsfolk finding faith, the exact subject of the intercession. Forgive us, if when we pray or sing "Send revival," the unuttered subtext is ever, "Send new people to our church!" Forgive us for reducing the revival prayer to nothing more than the slogan of a recruitment drive?

The Inter-Flow Across the Body

Returning to the body metaphor, we have seen that each congregation, as part of the body is not only valuable but has its unique function. But the metaphor goes much deeper than that. The life of the human body is sustained by that which flows <u>between</u> its parts. The circulatory, nervous and lymphatic systems work across every part of the body to supply, protect, empower and clean every part in order for it to function. Similarly, we shall see that within the congregational and denominational structure there is an active, living system already functioning seamlessly across it with no consideration of boundaries. We will also see how cross-congregational (or even cross-denominational) leadership is meant to work.

But more of that a little later, for now let's first go deeper in how we can really co-exist and co-operate together.

14. Being of One Breath

Living in Harmony

It's time to do a little bit more Bible study. I want to focus on one word – 'Harmony'. Dependent on which translation you use, you will read throughout the epistles, over and over again that the apostles exhort us to live in harmony with one another.

> *'Live in harmony with one another.'* [1]
> *'All of you be harmonious.'* [2]
> *'Live in harmony with each other.'* [3]
> *'Live in harmony by showing love for each other.'* [4]
> *'Binds us all together in perfect harmony.'* [5]
> *'Be diligent to keep the harmony of The Spirit in the bonds of peace.'* [6]

And this appeal to harmony is often conjoined with one to *'Live in peace.'* Peace and harmony going hand in hand, two different but closely interdependent ideas. I would suggest that over the centuries the Church has pursued peace at the expense of harmony. We may no longer shed each other's blood but is that only because we hold each other at a distance?

Let's first reflect on the fact that the instruction and encouragement to 'live in peace' does imply that there is a natural tendency <u>not</u> to live in peace. The absence of peace is conflict and even the most cursory investigation of Church history shows that we have been pretty good (or should it be bad) at conflict. We have seriously failed to live in peace, and have sadly resorted to shedding of blood. From the Thirty Years war across Europe,

---

[1] Romans 12 v 16
[2] 1 Peter 3 v 8
[3] 1 Corinthians 1 v 10
[4] Philippians 2 v 2
[5] Colossians 3 v 14
[6] Ephesians 4 v 3

through the English and American Civil Wars, to the troubles in Northern Ireland, wars have been fuelled by one part of God's Church fighting against another. How shameful of us. We all share the corporate guilt of ages past and present. It is no wonder those outside the Church can look-on in despair and question our integrity and love for one another.

'By this shall all men know that you are <u>not</u> my disciples – if you have conflict one with each other.'

I would like to suggest that we, the Church, have failed to 'live in peace' primarily because we didn't understand what 'live in harmony' meant. Sadly, this is still true today.

Phronema

Dependent upon which translation you favour, passages translated as 'live in harmony' may more commonly be rendered as an exhortation to 'be of the same mind'. The words or phrases that are usually translated thus are built from the root Phronema, typically either Homophron or Autophron, or their sub-derivations. Whilst Phronema does indeed mean 'mind' it is perhaps not the mind as you may think.

There are three Greek words typically translated in scripture as 'mind.' These are:

1. Psuche (from which we get Psyche) meaning a person's soul as opposed to their physical body or spirit. i.e. the inner person.

2. Nous (from which we get nous, i.e. common sense) meaning the organ of our mental perception. The mind that collects data from the senses and through reasoning makes decisions.

3.   Phronema (from which we get diaphragm) meaning our thoughts, feelings and desires. The source of which was considered to be, not the head, but the chest.

When the Bible says 'Be of one mind' it uses the word Phronema. This is also the same word that Paul uses when he says:

   'The mind set on the flesh'[1] and being, *'Carnally'* or *'Spiritually minded.'*[2]

In both passages we are exhorted to bring our 'mind' under control and in using Phronema Paul clarifies that he is not talking about our inner soul, nor our intellect, but our feelings desires and thoughts, which <u>can</u> be brought into line with the purposes of God or if left unchecked may lead us astray. These wayward thoughts and emotions are controllable.

But why diaphragm? With modern medical knowledge we understand that the diaphragm is simply the muscle that separated our chest from our abdomen. But in ancient times it was considered that part of your 'mind' was considered to be in the chest. It is a little like saying to a loved one that they are in your heart – anatomically impossible but we accept the idea. Now, consider the simple action of holding your breath which requires your brain to tell your diaphragm to stop flexing for a while. In so doing you stop breathing. Have you ever considered therefore that the lungs are the only vital organ you can choose to control? You can't stop your heart, liver, kidneys, or brain but you can stop your lungs, albeit temporarily, and to do so you use your diaphragm. I believe that this is the key linguistic reason that feelings, desires and thoughts are considered as being 'of the chest' or 'of the diaphragm' – it is in our ability to self-apply control to them.

---

[1] Romans 8 v 5
[2] Romans 8 vs 6 & 7

In being encouraged to live in harmony or to be 'of one mind', we are being asked to bring our Phronema into alignment together. If the word used had been either Psuche or Nous then it would mean we needed to get our inner convictions aligned or reach an intellect agreement.

But that is not the case, the word used is Phronema. You could say therefore acting in unity is not so much about being of one mind but of **being of One Breath**.

We can immediately see that 'harmony' or 'being of the same mind' is therefore not necessarily about changing our inner convictions, or reaching an intellectual agreement (or dare I say a doctrinal agreement). It is more about taking hold of our desires, thoughts and feelings and centring these on Christ. This is the essence of the second commandment, *'You shall love your neighbour as yourself.'* [1] Where we are commanded to act in love to each other and when we find that difficult, the source of that change is God.

'May God, who gives this patience and encouragement, help you live in complete <u>harmony</u> with each other, as is fitting for followers of Christ Jesus.' [2]

Phronemo and its derivations are used six times in the New Testament to mean 'of the same mind,' and always used in the context of how you <u>act</u> towards people.

'Bless those who persecute you; bless and do not curse. Rejoice with those who rejoice, and weep with those who weep. <u>Be of the same mind toward one another</u>. Do not set your mind on high things, but associate with the humble. Do not be wise in your own opinion. [3]

---

[1] Matthew 22 v 39
[2] Romans 15 v 5
[3] Romans 12 vs 14-16

'Let each of us please his neighbour for his good, leading to edification…. may the God of patience and comfort grant you to be like-minded toward one another.'[1]

In 2 Corinthians 13 v 11 the 'be of one mind' phrase is used in the context of rejoicing, comforting, living in love and peace, and how you greet one another. Then in Philippians 2 vs 1-8 it is used alongside being encouraging, comforting, loving, affectionate, sympathetic, joyful, humble, selfless and serving. None of these are about agreeing the same doctrinal position, nor about church governance, mission, or (insert the contentious topic of your choice). It is all about how we respond to each other when we are together. Being of one breath, being in harmony, is caring about each other even if you do not agree with them.

Sumphoneo

A second word that is also translated as harmony, is sumphoneo which I believe opens up an even more important meaning. Sumphoneo is defined in Strong's Concordance as: To be in harmony, to harmonize with, generally to agree together.

Note the 'phono' part of Sumphonia which means 'sound' or 'music.' Unsurprisingly, this is the word from which we get Symphony. A symphony is a beautiful piece of music that is made by a collection of very different instruments all being played together, in their own way, under the direction of a conductor.

No matter how much you try, if you blow a violin, bang a trumpet and pluck a drum, you won't get music. Each needs to be played in its own way. Also, if they all played what and when they wanted to, without reference to the conductor, the sound would be an atrocious cacophony. But each doing their own thing, under the leadership of the master, produces music.

---

[1] Romans 15 vs 2-5

154

It would be a disaster if each musician didn't concentrate on their own part but got distracted by what the other instruments were playing.

Consonance

But, of course, harmony is more than just music. A harmonious sound is made when two or more different notes are played at the same time. But not just any notes, they have to be the right notes played at the right time. We can't get away with "Playing all the right notes but not necessarily in the right order!"[1]

From the time of the ancient Greeks people have tried to understand why some combinations of notes give a pleasing, or 'Consonant' sound whereas others give a sound that is unpleasant, or 'Dissonant.' To this day, neurophysiologists[2] have tried, without much success, to understand how it affects the brain. The fact that it does is undeniable. Consonant harmony is pleasing to the ear, and I believe this holds an important message for us in considering unity in the One Church. As enjoyable as listening to a melody is, adding-in consonant harmony makes it so much more pleasing. Harmonics is the fullness of music.

Imagine if you were to get dressed in your finest dinner jacket or ballgown and to visit one of the grand concert halls. You take your seat in the stalls, and clap as the conductor arrives. You hold your beath in anticipation only to hear one note played. You would want your money back. You were expecting a symphony, a syn-phono, a collection of phonetics, or as we usually call it... music. Instead, you just got a sym-phoney!

It takes two notes to produce a harmonic. So, you can't have harmony without difference. Harmony cannot exist without difference. Without different instruments and notes you can't

[1] Morecambe and Wise with André Previn, 1971
[2] "Why harmony pleases the brain" by Lisa Grossman New Scientist 19 September 2011

have a symphony and without different people and different congregations you cannot have a harmonious co-existence.

In 1 Corinthians chapter 12 Pauls teaches on unity and diversity. We have already looked at much of this chapter, but notice what he says immediately afterward. In the very first verse of chapter 13 we read that if we do not act in love we will,

'Become sounding brass or a clanging cymbal.' [1]

If we only ever read this most famous of Biblical chapters as a standalone, we can easily miss the link between disunity and discordant sound.

Ya-Had

Looking into the Old Testament we find a Hebrew word translated harmony or unity, particularly in Psalm 133:1

'How wonderful and pleasant it is when brothers live together in harmony! For it is as precious as the anointing oil that was poured over Aaron's head. It is as refreshing as the dew from Mount Hermon that falls on the mountains of Zion for there the Lord has bestowed the blessing of life forevermore.' [2]

The Hebrew Ya-Had literally means 'together' – that is physically together in the same place. Of the 141 times it is used in the Old Testament it is usually simply translated as 'together.'

The emphasis of the Hebrew word is again not about agreement, but about physical action. The nation of Israel was made up of twelve diverse tribes and yet the physical act of being together, typically at one of the feasts, is described as both wonderful and pleasant.

---

[1] 1 Corinthians 13 v 1
[2] Psalm 133 vs 1-3

In conclusion, when we read that God, *'Does not want us to be in disorder but in harmony and peace,'*[1] we see that peace (i.e. the removal of conflict) and harmony are achieved by:

Being of the same breath, choosing to take our emotions and desires in hand for the sake of unity,

Playing our part at the right time, under the guidance of the conductor (the Holy Spirit), ignoring what the others are doing,

Physically meeting together, which is both wonderful and pleasant.

We have discovered a lot of important truths together, now let's turn our attention to understanding how these can be implemented within the One Church.

---

[1] 1 Corinthians 4 v 13

Challenge 4: Understanding the One Church

15. What Exactly is Church?

<u>Are you the Church?</u>

There is a much-loved children's story by P.D. Eastman called 'Are You My Mother?' If you are not familiar with the book let me outline it for you. A little bird hatches from an egg when the mother bird is not on the nest. The little bird then wanders around the farmyard, going up to several different animals asking each of them, "Are you my mother?" The animals gently explain that they are <u>not</u> its mother, so the baby bird has to keep looking. Don't worry, it does have a happy ending when the little chick eventually finds its mother.

I am indebted to Bible-teacher Dalton Thomas for presenting the idea that this book is an analogy for how the outside world looks at the Church.[1] The spiritually lost people around us are looking for Jesus, even though most wouldn't admit it. Somehow they know that we are the representation of Jesus on earth, so they inevitably come to us, look at us intently and ask, "Are you the Church?"

They look at our carefully orchestrated seeker-friendly gospel services and ask, "Is that the Church?"

They look at the glorious architecture of Saint Peter's Basilica in the Vatican and ask, "Is that the Church?"

They look at the multi-media mega-church in its purpose-built five-thousand-seater auditorium and ask, "Is that the Church?"

---

[1] Dalton Thomas in Origins, part of the Maranatha Bible Study, FAImission.org

They look at those gathering each week in the local school hall for worship followed by tea and biscuits and ask, "Is that the Church?"

They look at the tireless workers out on the streets, caring for the homeless and running the food banks and ask, "Is that the Church?"

They look at the missionaries in the unreached parts of the world and ask, "Is that the Church?"

Which of these is the correct answer? It is here that the analogy with the chicken-book breaks down. Whilst the chick is seeking the one true answer, the challenge for us is quite the opposite.

We saw in the last chapter that every part of the Christian Church is both important and valuable. So, unlike the ever-seeking chick, we have to consider that all of the representations we just listed are indeed 'Church.'

But what do we mean by Church? Firstly, we will go over a few basics, probably stuff you already know. But then we will look at a couple of Biblical passages from which we can gain an important insight on how Paul saw the Church.

The Church is not a Building

The first thing to say about Church is to state a few things that it is not. Church is not a building, nor a religious service, nor an organisation. The Church is a body of Christian believers. The Church is people – always and only people. We've been preaching this truth for decades (probably centuries) but it is so easy to slip back into the visible reality, rather than the eternal truth.

All too often I use the lazy shorthand and say that I am, "Going to church," or might invite someone to, "Come to church with me." We don't go to church, the church gathers! But in all honesty, I don't think I've ever invited someone to <u>meet</u> my church – only ever to <u>come to</u> my church. It is one thing knowing the truth, it is something else to allow it to pervade our vocabulary – let alone our behaviour.

I am sure you won't have missed the irony that having stated categorically for years that the Church is not a building we suddenly didn't have access to our premises throughout the Covid-19 lockdowns. It's as though God issued the Church with the challenge,

"You may have said it, but let's see if you really believe it."

During the lockdowns I attended several online seminars presented by leaders of national inter-church ministries. The common message they reported was that many congregations had effectively gone into hibernation waiting for things to return to normal. Conversely, some congregations had taken up the Covid challenge and thrived at finding new and meaningful ways to connect with each other and their communities unencumbered by the needs of a physical premise. I even heard of one congregation that took active steps to <u>not return</u> to their former buildings and/or meetings post-lockdown.

But before we move on, the Bible does make it clear that the Church does need to meet...

'And let us consider one another in order to stir up love and good works, not forsaking the assembling of ourselves together, as is the manner of some, but exhorting one another, and so much the more as you see the day approaching.' [1]

This is a stark warning that Christians <u>must</u> meet together in order to encourage each other into both love and good works. In order to meet together we need to have a place to meet. In the early Church that would have been in homes. Perhaps lockdown

---

[1] Hebrews 10 v 24 – 25

has instilled a desire to return to something akin to that. And let's also recognise that not having a building for a time might just be practise for, as we have seen, the situation to come when we enter the end-times.

But for now – Church is <u>not</u> a building.

The Church is not a Meeting

Neither, is the Church a meeting. Again, I have fallen into the lazy lexicon of saying things like, "Church was great last Sunday." Instead, I should have said, "My church had a great service last Sunday." After all, the Church is great every day, even when it isn't gathered together in one place.

Consider, if the Church acts to meet the needs of the community, be it at a homeless shelter, a mothers-and-toddlers group, a youth club, or a jumble-sale, is it not still <u>being</u> Church? These are not extra things that the Church does – these are core expressions of being His people.

Let's go further, if Christians gather socially, is this also still being Church? For some, an active demonstration of Christian love one for another will be a meeting for coffee and cake, or for beer and a curry, or for a gourmet meal. For some they will meet to play sport, to walk their dogs, to climb a mountain, to visit the swimming pool, the cinema, the bowling alley or the museum. Simply spending quality time together is as much being Church as worshipping together. It may come as a surprise, but we are expected to enjoy each other's company!

We are Church as we serve the community or meet socially, but that is not the whole story. Whilst Church isn't a service (and by extension nor a specific liturgy) meeting together to worship Jesus and celebrate The Eucharist is nonetheless a command as we read in Luke:

"And He took bread, gave thanks and broke it, and gave it to them, saying, "This is My body which is given for you; do this in remembrance of Me."" [1]

The Church is not an Organisation

Thirdly, the Church is not an organisation. Lazy shorthand may allow someone to be described as "working for the church," or as being "high up in the church," but if the Church is truly just the people, then neither of these phrases make sense.

I know some will accuse me of being pedantic and not realistic to the needs of a complex church system these days. In response to that valid accusation, may I direct us, once again, to history. As we saw in the early Church was a very flat organisation, decidedly not the way you would structure a world-changing movement, especially one that numbered into the millions even then. Perhaps it was the notable absence of organisation and the prominent role of relationships that was as visible a testimony to the work of the Holy Spirit in the early Church as were signs and wonders.

So, we are clear then. Not a building, not a service and not an organisation.

So what is it?

Ekklesia

When we read the English word 'Church' in the Bible it has been translated from the Greek word Ekklesia which means, "The gathering of those summoned." This word, together with its grammatical sub-derivations, is used 228 times in the New Testament, largely being translated (in the KJV) as either church or assembly.

---

[1] Luke 22 v 19

It has been taught by some that the Ekklesia was an ancient Greek term to mean the governmental body that ran a city. The link has then been made that the Church has been called-out to be God's government on earth and be active in building His kingdom. This is a significant stretch to how the term was originally employed.

The Encyclopaedia Britannica gives a good unbiased insight into the ancient Greek Ekklesia. It was a body which had existed since around 600BC but by New Testament times had become meaningless under the domination of the Roman empire. The word described how decision-making happened in a local metropolitan area, in ancient Greek society. The Ekklesia, made up of the entire male adult populous of a city, would occasionally be summoned for the purpose of discussing and then voting on a matter. The Ekklesia did not have the authority to choose what topics to vote upon, only to make decisions on the choices presented before it by the government. It was therefore a decision-making body only in the sense of giving local assent to a government recommendation. In either approving or rejecting a decision, its role was simply in order to include 'representation of the people,' and as such was akin to a mini-local-referendum. Agreement would then give validity to the laws to which they had given their consent. Following Roman occupation, the local populous was no longer invited to be involved in such decision-making, and the term fell into disuse.[1]

But Jesus chose this word to describe His people. Translating these historical facts into the Christian context, we can see a certain logic in the use of the word. Firstly, let's consider the literal definition, 'The gathering of those summoned.'

1. **Gathering.**
    Notwithstanding the fact that we just decided that the Church isn't a meeting, you can't have an Ekklesia (a church) without actually meeting together. It would

---

[1] "Ecclesia ancient Greek assembly" Encyclopaedia Britannica. From Britannica.com

be lexicographically meaningless. Church = Gathered. As to when and where, that is open to discussion.

2. Summoned.
The people who are to gather are those who have been summoned by a higher authority. In the Church context that is clearly God. Notice, that they are not invited, nor encouraged, but summoned. To which we should be at pains to comply.

In addition, we can also gain insight by considering how the Ekklesia functioned in ancient Greece.

3. Inclusivity
All people were summoned, (I will deliberately ignore the male-only criteria) and so we can confer that all believers are automatically enrolled within the Ekklesia.

4. Equality
Without trying to make a political point about democracy, I simply want to make the observation that everyone had an equal say. All members of the Ekklesia were equally important; no one was more important than any other.

5. Locality
The jurisdiction of the Ekklesia wasn't national but expressly local. Again, this mirrors the specific local identity of a church, as we saw in the early Church. But let's not forget that as the Church we can also pray for change on a national or global basis.

6. Focus
The Ekklesia did not have the authority to go off-piste and debate meaningless topics. It had to stay within the area that it had been convened to decide upon. Likewise, the Church is not invited to make-up its own

doctrine but to stay within that which has already been proscribed. This was very much what we saw evidenced within the early Church with its focus on faithfully passing on of the Apostles teaching.

7. Authority
Despite the constraint on the scope of authority stated above, the decisions made by the Ekklesia were nonetheless final and binding. As the Church of God, we are invited to partner with Him, in His authority.

8. Consent
The whole point of the Ekklesia was to confer consensual self-governance (in the context of law-enforcement) within a locality. Once the decision was made, they consented to live with it. Likewise, the Church is a body of people consenting to live together under the laws of God.

I think that is probably enough on the word Ekklesia. I am sure you can find dozens of other worthy discussions on the topic but I hope this has given some insight as to why Jesus borrowed the word to describe His people.

Now onto something that hopefully you may find new.

Who's Who (Pauline edition)

Have you ever noticed that at the end of some of his letters the Apostle Paul spends a few verses writing greetings to and from various people and churches? You can see this at the end of his first letter to the Corinthian Church[1] and most notably at the end of his letter to the Church in Rome.[2] It is easy to gloss over these 'greetings' passages as being only relevant for the time they were written, but I believe they hold a powerful truth for us today.

---

[1] 1 Corinthians 16 vs 5-19
[2] Romans 16 vs 3-15

First, we'll read them both and note what is included. Then we'll reflect on what that teaches us about the nature of Church as Paul saw it. Let's start with the Corinthian passage from chapter 16 verses 5 to 19:

'Now I will come to you when I pass through Macedonia (for I am passing through Macedonia). And it may be that I will remain, or even spend the winter with you, that you may send me on my journey, wherever I go. For I do not wish to see you now on the way; but I hope to stay a while with you, if the Lord permits. But I will tarry in Ephesus until Pentecost. For a great and effective door has opened to me, and there are many adversaries. And if Timothy comes, see that he may be with you without fear; for he does the work of the Lord, as I also do. Therefore let no one despise him. But send him on his journey in peace, that he may come to me; for I am waiting for him with the brethren. Now concerning our brother Apollos, I strongly urged him to come to you with the brethren, but he was quite unwilling to come at this time; however, he will come when he has a convenient time. Watch, stand fast in the faith, be brave, be strong. Let all that you do be done with love. I urge you, brethren—you know the household of Stephanas, that it is the firstfruits of Achaia, and that they have devoted themselves to the ministry of the saints— that you also submit to such, and to everyone who works and labours with us. I am glad about the coming of Stephanas, Fortunatus, and Achaicus, for what was lacking on your part they supplied. For they refreshed my spirit and yours. Therefore, acknowledge such men. The churches of Asia greet you. Aquila and Priscilla greet you heartily in the Lord, with the church that is in their house.'

Paul wrote this, his first letter to the Corinthian Church from his prison cell in Rome and in these closing verses makes mention of Macedonia and Ephesus. That makes four places: Rome, Corinth, Macedonia and Ephesus spread across four different countries.

He mentions young Timothy and warns the church to not look down on him, as well as his fellow apostolic teacher Apollos whom he actively encourages to come. He also mentions Stephanus, Fortunatus and Achaicus.

He talks of the churches of Asia, a wide geographic area and also the church that meets in the house of Aquila and Priscilla.

Let's compare that to the greetings listed at the end of the letter to the Romans, chapter 16 verses 1 to 15:

'I commend to you Phoebe our sister, who is a servant of the church in Cenchrea, that you may receive her in the Lord in a manner worthy of the saints, and assist her in whatever business she has need of you; for indeed she has been a helper of many and of myself also. Greet Priscilla and Aquila, my fellow workers in Christ Jesus, who risked their own necks for my life, to whom not only I give thanks, but also all the churches of the Gentiles. Likewise greet the church that is in their house. Greet my beloved Epaenetus, who is the first fruits of Achaia to Christ. Greet Mary, who laboured much for us. Greet Andronicus and Junia, my countrymen and my fellow prisoners, who are of note among the apostles, who also were in Christ before me. Greet Amplias, my beloved in the Lord. Greet Urbanus, our fellow worker in Christ, and Stachys, my beloved. Greet Apelles, approved in Christ. Greet those who are of the household of Aristobulus. Greet Herodion, my countryman. Greet those who are of the household of Narcissus who are in the Lord. Greet Tryphena and Tryphosa, who have laboured in the Lord. Greet the beloved Persis, who laboured much in the Lord. Greet Rufus, chosen in the Lord, and his mother and mine. Greet Asyncritus, Phlegon, Hermas, Patrobas, Hermes, and the brethren who are with them. Greet Philologus and Julia, Nereus and his sister, and Olympas, and all the saints who are with them.'

Here Paul again makes mention of both Timothy and Priscilla and Aquila. He also names Phoebe, from the church of Cenchrea, and Epaenetus from the church in Achaia.

Then we hear a long list of names. Some he calls his fellow prisoners (i.e. Andronicus and Junia). Some have Roman names (e.g. Urbanus) some have Greek names (e.g. Stachys) and some are described as being Paul's fellow countrymen (e.g Herodion). There are those described not as a person but as those of a household (i.e. Aristobulus and Narcissus), which may mean they had some level of Roman nobility.

Then there is a list of people whose names live on within the pages of the inspired word of God, and yet we will never know anything about them. Mary, Tryphena, Tryphosa, Persis, Rufus, Apelles, Asyncritus, Phlegon, Hermas, Patrobas, Hermes, Amplias, Philologus, Olympas, Julia, Nereus and his sister. And finally, Paul gives a catch-all, others whose names not even he could recall, and are described simply as 'the saints who are with them.'

I don't know about you, but I have tended to glaze over when reading these passages. But what a mistake. This extensive, and easily overlooked, rollcall has an important purpose. What is Paul doing in these two passages? He is quite simply describing the Church as it was in his day. And more than that, by naming them in scripture he is legitimising them all.

So, let's take a closer look at the Church as Paul saw it.

There are geographically diverse churches listed, including some he described by a wide area (i.e. Asia) implying several churches in relationship together; also city churches including what we might today call the mega church at Ephesus. This concurs with our exploration of geography from a previous chapter.

He addresses gender (both male and female are listed), race (Roman, Greek and Jew), age (i.e. Timothy) and social status with some being members of sizeable and wealthy Roman households, others being as low as you can get, prisoners.

Then there are those described as workers with him. In our modern parlance we might describe these as those with 'a ministry' or as parachurch workers. Some were well known at the time (e.g. Apollos) but others largely unknown.

Can you see what Paul is doing in these greetings? He is saying they are all equally valid. They are all legitimate. They are all part of the One Church.

In these passages he treats a regional group of churches (Asia), a city-church (Ephesus) and a house church (Aquilla and Priscilla) as well as parachurch ministers (Stephanus) as all the same. In the Western Church, particularly with its Greek-mindset, the need for structure twitches and says they are clearly not the same. Something inside wants to put the house church within the city church and the city church within the regional network. We like that sort of pyramid. It feels neat. Small inside bigger inside the largest like a set of Russian dolls, but that is expressly not what Paul is doing. Poor Andronicus, chained to the prison wall in Rome, gets the same name-check as 'all the churches in Asia.'

How can this be? Because they are all valid expressions of the One Church that Paul witnessed.

It can be quite a mind-shift, but also a transformational one if we are able to allow the need for structure to dissolve from us. We know the Church is not a building, is not a service, nor an organisation. It certainly doesn't have an organisational chart. You cannot write the Church down on a sheet of paper, there is no blueprint available to us.

What we do know is that the Church is the multi-size, multi-gender, multi-race, multi-status, multi-role, melting pot that Christ specifically designed His body to be. We would be wise to accept every part of His body as being both valid and vital.

16. "You are A Holy Nation"

A Brief Recap

We have seen that despite us creating thousands of different denominations God considers that He has, against all the observable evidence, just One Church. To be able to accept this, we first needed to reject the traditional excuses and be open-minded enough to allow His truth to become our reality.

Next, we considered that to decide if a group of believers is Christian, there are two options. Firstly, we can rely on the witness of the Holy Spirit within us to guide us; if we can correctly discern His voice, then we will be assured of making the right judgement, every time. However, we need to recognise that our prejudices and traditional views may sometimes make hearing His voice more difficult than it really ought to be. If we need a doctrinal checklist, we are probably safest to use the Nicene Creed (some things were omitted but nothing crucial to salvation). We can, of course, use both methods.

Next, we saw that despite these common foundational beliefs there are still huge differences, not only in style, structure and practice but also on strongly polarising topics that on face-value would appear to create irreconcilable divisions between us. We have also seen that even in this situation, we are commanded to not judge (i.e. condemn) but to act in humility, love and grace toward those with opposing views.

Crucially, we have also seen that we mustn't compromise, nor water-down our personally held views, but to graciously and lovingly hold firm to them, even though other Christians may disagree. We have also seen that there is a unity possible despite our individuality and that as a body we are to celebrate our differences not to try and annul them.

With our natural eyes we may see a fragmented Church, but with our spiritual eyes we can see that there is just One Church made up of a diversity of individual congregations. How does this work in practice? Let's look at the Biblical principle to see how.

One Nation under God

In addressing the Church, the Apostle Peter stated that, *'You are a Holy Nation.'* [1] In so doing he was referencing the same words spoken by God through Moses to the nation of Israel.

'"And you shall be to Me a kingdom of priests and a holy nation." These are the words which you shall speak to the children of Israel' [2]

In addressing the Church as a Holy Nation (which we understand means to be grafted into the Holy Nation of Israel); the One Church and the Biblical nation of Israel are inextricably linked. The similarities are stronger than you may think.

From its inception the nation of Israel has had its own built-in differences. It is a nation made up of twelve individual and very different tribes – the twelve tribes descended from the twelve sons of Jacob (re-named Israel). Shortly before his death Jacob gave a prophetic blessing and/or warning to each of his sons. Each son's blessing was appropriate to them, and referenced their character and actions which, as the tribal patriarch, would set the course of the future destiny of the tribe. This blessing therefore was not just personal to the son but also a statement for their descendants, over the subsequent centuries.

'All these are the twelve tribes of Israel, and this is what their father spoke to them. And he blessed them; he blessed each one according to his own blessing.' [3]

---

[1] 1 Peter 2 v 9
[2] Exodus 19 v 6
[3] Genesis 49 v 28

172

Wind the clock forward 210 years. The sons of Jacob have died, and their descendants have grown into twelve identifiable and independent tribes each numbering in the tens of thousands.[1] Then, just like the death-bed blessings that Jacob gave to each of his sons, we see this repeated as Moses gives a prophetic blessing and/or warning particular to each individual tribe shortly before his own demise.[2]

Jacob and Moses both gave a tribal blessing. One at the tribe's infancy, the other after they had matured. But note something very important. Both sets of blessings came before the nation of Israel existed.

Let me clarify that statement. In their flight from Egypt the Children of Israel were never described as a nation. God promises that *'I will make of you a great nation'* [3] and, *'I will make of you a nation greater and mightier than they.'* [4] and even states that the surrounding nations will recognise their divine nationhood,

'Surely, I have taught you statutes and judgments… be careful to observe them… in the sight of the peoples who will… say, 'Surely this great nation is a wise and understanding people.' [5]

All of these promises are in the future tense, to be fulfilled through the conquest and settlement of Canaan under Joshua. The first time God unequivocally named Israel as a nation was in response to their rebellion:

'The anger of the Lord was hot against Israel; and He said, "Because this nation has transgressed My covenant…"' [6]

During the wilderness years they are either addressed as the Children of Israel (i.e. a related people group) or as the Twelve

---

[1] Numbers 1 vs 20 - 46
[2] Deuteronomy 33 vs 6 - 25
[3] Exodus 31 v 10
[4] Numbers 14 v 12
[5] Deuteronomy 4 v 5 & 6
[6] Judges 2 v 20

Tribes. Meaning that the Exodus was tribal. We see this clearly when Moses counts the people shortly after their miraculous departure. You may be forgiven in thinking that his census was simply a count of how many people had escaped Egypt. That is partially true but notice: the census was conducted by tribe.

> "Then Moses and Aaron... assembled all the congregation together... and they recited their ancestry by families, by their fathers' houses... so he numbered them." [1]

This tribal structure also dictated how the people camped in the wilderness.

> "Everyone of the children of Israel shall camp by his own standard, beside the emblems of his father's house." [2]

And yet, even in this camp of twelve tribes,[3] Moses was instructed by God to address the people as a single entity, "The Children of Israel." [4]

So, which was it? Was Moses leading twelve independent tribes or one cohesive body, (though not a nation as they possessed no land)? Have you ever considered that every time Moses used the expression "Children of Israel" that those hearing it might not have been in whole-hearted agreement? Let me speculate for fun. Consider an aged warrior from the tribe of Simeon who, on hearing Moses, says under his breath to his friends in private,

"Yeah, I know that this Children of Israel thing is technically correct, but I'm a Simeonite. Look at the flag where I camp – Simeonite. That is the cause I fight for, that is who I'll defend to my dying breath. That is who I am!"

---

[1] Numbers 1 vs 17-19
[2] Numbers 2 v 2
[3] Numbers 2 vs 1-34
[4] There are numerous occurrences. I offer the following examples: Exodus 16 vs 9 & 11; Exodus 19 v 3; Numbers 5 vs 2, 5 &12

I am just speculating, of course, I don't know how a Simeonite warrior might have thought, but please note the Biblical facts. The tribal identity persisted throughout the wilderness years, throughout the conquest and settling of Canaan, right through to the divided kingdom and their subsequent exile.

What is even more staggering is that this tribal structure is eternal. Jesus told his disciples that in the regeneration when the Son of Man will sit on His glorious throne, they would sit on twelve thrones judging the twelve tribes of Israel.[1] Then later in Revelation we see twelve tribes listed, making up the 144,000-strong remnant of Israel.[2]

We are safe to say that the tribal identity came first. It also persisted long after the nation was established because tribal allegiance was more than just a statement of hereditary, it was each Israelite's principal identity. See how these twelve tribes were described as one people long before the nation of Israel existed. And see how that nation was then continually described as twelve tribes. Is there a meaning to this identity schizophrenia?

Dual Identity

God told Moses to speak of One Nation when the visible reality around him suggested that there were in fact twelve separate, though related, identities. This is not too dissimilar to what we see in the Church today. God speaks of One Church despite the evidence we see on the ground in our towns and cities. I feel there is something important we can learn from this.

God's concept of One Nation clearly includes scope for a lot of variety. The Children of Israel had variety built in. Members of the tribe of, for example, Reuben, knew they were both Reubenites as well as Israelites. This form of dual identity persists

---

[1] Matthew 19 v 28
[2] Revelation 7 vs 4-8

today. I consider myself to be both English and British (and in some contexts might describe myself as European). I have friends who are proud to call themselves Yorkshiremen, as well as English. I know of many people in America for whom the State of their birth forms as much of their identity as does their allegiance to the American flag. I have worked with Dutch colleagues from the northern part of The Netherlands who freely describe themselves as Frieslanders.

In some way these, let's call them 'local identities,' feel more personal than the overall national one. We can stand up proud of the overall national identity when it comes to patriotism, or for the defence of the nation, or sharing in past glorious history or in sporting victories (should they ever happen). But it is the local identity that perhaps says more about us personally.

In the examples I just shared with you it would not be unusual to describe some of the people involved by using terms such as,
"Yorkshiremen are like…",
"Texans are like…", or
"Frieslanders are like…".

Indeed, it wouldn't even be offensive to insert into these expressions a negative stereotype, provided that it is a widely held view of persons from that area. For example, if I were to say that, "Yorkshiremen are blunt and to the point," this wouldn't be considered an insult, even though I am sure many of them are as sensitive and tactful as anyone else. In some ways the stereotypical 'local' identity can be a badge of honour.

Local identity matters. To some it matters a lot. If you spend any time in Scotland, Quebec or the Basque Country you will see that for some the local identity is vastly more important than the national one, to the extent they crave independence from it.

One Before God

Let's look a little deeper. In the Old Testament we see that when God addressed His people, it was always as a <u>Nation</u> – not individual tribes. This principle was built into the newly formed nation of Israel by having the priestly tribe of Levi liberally scattered across all of the tribal territories.[1] Consider Leviticus 23 where God commands the <u>Nation</u> to gather to celebrate the weekly Sabbath plus the seasonal feasts of Passover; First Fruits; Pentecost (Weeks); The Day of Atonement; Trumpets; and finally, Tabernacles.

'The LORD spoke to Moses, saying, "Speak to the children of Israel, and say to them: 'The feasts of the LORD, which you shall proclaim to be holy convocations, these are My feasts.'"' [2]

I know that the Church has largely forgotten these feasts (or worse substituted an alternative ecclesiastical calendar), and the rediscovery of them is another subject outside of the scope of this book, but the point I am making is that God's command to celebrate was to the <u>Children of Israel</u> (i.e. one entity), not to the individual tribes. And this command was despite the fact that, at this point, the nation of Israel (as defined by possessing land) did not exist as such. They were, in all practical reality, twelve tribes. We see this principle echoed later when the national identity had been established, and yet the tribal structure remained. Look at when Solomon announced he was going to build a temple.

'Behold, I am building a temple for the name of the Lord my God, to dedicate it to Him, to burn before Him sweet incense, for the continual showbread, for the burnt offerings, morning and evening, on the Sabbaths, on the New Moons, and on the set feasts of the Lord our God. This is an ordinance forever to Israel.' [3]

---

[1] Numbers 35 vs 1 -8
[2] Leviticus 23 vs 1-2
[3] 2 Chronicles 2 v 4

He clearly says he is doing it because it was an ordinance to Israel, the nation. Then later, when the temple is ready for its consecration we read,

> 'Now Solomon assembled the elders of Israel and all the <u>heads of the tribes</u>, the chief fathers of the children of Israel, to King Solomon in Jerusalem, that they might bring up the ark of the covenant of the Lord from the City of David, which is Zion. Therefore, <u>all the men of Israel</u> assembled with King Solomon at the feast.' [1]

Notice how, 350 years after God gave the divine decree to celebrate the feasts, and after decades of united national kingly rule, the tribal identity is still firmly in place. Despite this, Solomon's prayer of dedication over the temple and the people only references the single nation of Israel.

So, in the Old Testament there appears to be no tension between these two identities: the tribal and a national. We see that when they were gathering **before God, they acted as one.** Perhaps we can take this as a principle for the One Church. When it comes to gathering before God, or worshipping, our 'local' tribal identity is meaningless. We will have to define what we mean by that local identity, but more on that later.

<u>One to the Outside World</u>

The second key learning point we could take from the National of Israel is that in times of war they <u>fought</u> as <u>One</u> <u>Nation</u>. In the face of an enemy the primary tribal allegiance was trumped by the national need.

> 'When you are on the verge of battle... the priest shall... speak to the people. And he shall say to them, "<u>Hear, O Israel:</u> Today you are on the verge of battle with your enemies. Do not let your heart faint, do not be afraid, and do not tremble or be terrified

---

[1] 1 Kings 8 vs 1 - 2a

because of them; for the LORD your God is He who goes with you, to fight for you against your enemies, to save you." [1]

Again, this word is given to a tribally structured assembly in the wilderness, long before the nation existed in a physical sense. Notice that the priest is to say to the army on the eve of battle, "Hear O Israel...". They were addressed as a unified fighting force. This was especially the case during the conquest of Canaan. See how Joshua addressed his army as a single entity.

'So Joshua said to the children of Israel, "Come here, and hear the words of the LORD your God." And Joshua said, "By this you shall know that the living God is among you, and that He will without fail drive out from before you the Canaanites and the Hittites and the Hivites and the Perizzites and the Girgashites and the Amorites and the Jebusites."' [2]

This was despite the fact that only days earlier Moses had given his deathbed tribe-by-tribe blessings.[3] Later, at the end of the conquest of the land, Joshua then gathered the nation together specifically to restore the tribal identities in the distribution of their inheritances.

"Now the whole congregation of the children of Israel assembled together at Shiloh, and set up the tabernacle of meeting there. And the land was subdued before them.... Then Joshua cast lots for them in Shiloh before the Lord, and there Joshua divided the land to the children of Israel according to their divisions." [4]

We can see therefore that in times of war or conquest, the tribes fought for each another, without question. **To the outside world, they acted as one.** Again, we could take this principle for the Church today.

---

[1] Deuteronomy 20 vs 2-4
[2] Joshua 3 vs 9-10
[3] Deuteronomy 33
[4] Joshua 18 vs 1 & 10

179

A Church made of Tribes

The tribal motif did of course affect their everyday lives. It dictated where they lived and worked, whom they married, and countless other day-to-day choices. In today's ecclesiastical language we could even say that **they fellowshipped only within their own tribe**.

In scripture we read Jacob, Moses, Jesus and John all referring to the nation of Israel specifically as '*The twelve tribes.*' This isn't just linguistic shorthand; it is vitally important to our understanding of identity. If one physical holy nation (Israel) is made up of multiple tribes, does it not follow that one spiritual holy nation (the One Church) is also made up of multiple tribes. If so, then maybe we can consider different church strands as simply tribes within the national whole? This sounds very plausible to me.

If so, it would follow that in our corporate response before God, our worship, there <u>is</u> just One Church. If we consider ourselves as merely tribes within this One Church (i.e. one holy nation) then we have a structure, a tribe/nation model, that readily accommodates variety. Even though we may disagree on doctrine or practice - **Before God we <u>are</u> one.**

But if we accept the tribe/nation model it also follows that 'to the outside world we are one.' Such a belief might be a lot harder to implement and sadly we must confess we have patently failed to act as one for centuries. Now is the time for that to end, now is the time to present a truly united front in the midst of the spiritual battles around us. If we are to embrace the idea that, **to the outside world we are one**, it will require a change in heart for most of us.

It is acceptable for us to hold on to a tribal identity, without undermining the fact that together we are one holy nation, One Church. This should especially be true in in our acts of worship and how we are seen by the outside world.

At first sight, embracing the tribe/nation model feels a little like the church-global/church-local model that I poo-pooed in an earlier chapter of this book. Similar, yes but there is a fundamental difference. The church-global/church-local ideology was, in my opinion, a convenient excuse that allowed me to ignore what any other Christian group did, said or believed. It gave me the option to claim that what 'they' did was 'nothing to do with me,' and leave it up to God to sort them out. The tribe/nation model is very different. It actively requires us to stand alongside, to worship alongside, to fight alongside, those of differing identities, including those with whom we do not agree. If we can crack this, then we will actively demonstrate His love to the world. We worship and fight together, even if we don't fellowship together.

Let me give you a hypothetical example. Let's imagine a town with two churches. We will call one of them St. Cuthbert's (i.e. church C), and we will call the other St. Dominican's (i.e. church D). St. Cuthbert's believes in preaching the gospel, morning noon and night. No dilution, no compromise – let's even say they preach 'hellfire and brimstone'. I am exaggerating for effect, you understand. Now St. Dominican's is different. They have a very active social outreach programme whereby they feed the homeless and help families in debt. They have a drug rehabilitation programme and such like. Crucially, (and this was the point of tension) they did all this social action without preaching the gospel to those whose needs they were meeting. This infuriated St. Cuthbert's who would question the whole point of social outreach if they didn't tell anyone the good news of salvation. St Dominican's felt that to have such an attitude would not exhibit the self-sacrificial love that Christ taught us, and that it would be wrong to only help those who had responded to their preaching. You get the idea – polarised views on the axis of The Social Gospel. Again, I am not going to make any personal view on the subject.

If these two churches truly embraced the tribe/nation model it would look like this. Those at St. Cuthbert's would actively

181

celebrate the work that St. Dominican's was doing, both in their own pulpit but also to the outside world. They would support it practically, financially and encourage volunteers from within their own congregation to go and help if they felt so called. In the course of their very active evangelistic work, they would not hesitate to refer needy people to one of St. Dominican's programmes without fear of losing potential converts from their own pews. St. Dominican's, for their part, fully understanding of their own limitations, would celebrate all that St. Cuthbert's was able to do; not only from their own pulpit but also to the outside world. Without taking their eye off the good work they were doing they would invite St. Cuthbert's to come and share the gospel, without restriction, in whatever way they felt appropriate, again without fear of losing potential converts from their own pews.

It's not a perfect example, but I hope it gives you an idea of two churches, choosing not to focus on their differences but rather to work together, each bringing their A-game to the battle. Each playing to their strengths.

If you were comfortable with this reasonably tame example, ask yourself how you would have reacted if I had described St. Cuthbert's and St. Dominican's as holding differing views on women in leadership, or on the gifts of the Holy Spirit, or on abortion, euthanasia, vaccination, alcohol, gay marriage, infant baptism, overt political allegiance, or the authority of the Pope? These are some of the real-life issues that divide us.

We all need to find our tribe, our place of belonging, with those who share our beliefs, particularly on divisive issues. This is part of our Christian identity. However, once we are safe within our tribe, we then must stand alongside those in other tribes that may hold opposing views. To do so, we'll need a huge dose of love, grace and humility. Only then will we present to the world God's loving, accepting, sacrificial, One Church nation. But what exactly is a tribe within the context of the Church? Is it my congregation or my denomination? Let's find out.

17. Finding Your Tribe

There were twelve tribes in the nation of Israel. So, when considering the Church as being 'tribal' the first thought I had was: Wouldn't it be neat if there were twelve church tribes.

Let me be clear, I am not saying there <u>are</u> twelve church tribes and that the 22,400 denominations or 4.1million congregations that currently exist somehow need to be shoe-horned into one of twelve predefined boxes. I'm not hung up on the need for there to be just twelve. God is omniscient and can cope with twelve thousand just as easily as with twelve, although I can't help but think that it would be somewhat pleasing if there were twelve distinct tribes within His Church.

For my next trick, I will now attempt to collapse thousands of denominations into just twelve broad groupings and shall do so in two very different ways.

A word of warning before I start. The results are not particularly pleasing, but my inner nerdiness meant I had to get this idea out of the way before I could then embrace the revelation which then came. You can either join me on these somewhat fruitless arithmetic and historical journeys, or skip forward to page 190 and pick up there. The choice is yours.

<u>Tribes based on present-day size.</u>

My first attempt was a purely arithmetic exercise. My plan was to consider the number of denominational members globally. In so doing I wasn't trying to force all these denominations into just twelve pots, I was looking to find out if they somehow already existed. I soon realised that I would need to define the eleven largest groups, not twelve because there would need to be a sizeable Miscellaneous pot at the end.

It wasn't as easy a task as I had first envisaged. As there are 2.5 billion Christians in the world today, mathematically that should break down into eleven pots of 200 million or so. If only things were that straightforward. Around half of all of those who name themselves as Christian are within the Catholic Church, plus a relatively minor 18 million non-Latin-rite Catholics which for this purpose I considered to be a sub-group. We have our first pot – and a very large one at that. This means the remaining 10 pots now can be around 100 million each. The next largest group are the Pentecostals at 280 million. Whilst this is made up of many, many, individual organisational strands, I felt that as the core beliefs, style and structure are broadly so similar it was justifiable to keep them as one. Next comes the 220 million Eastern Orthodox. This includes around 40 separate churches, including the more well-known Greek Orthodox and Russian Orthodox churches. As three quarters of the members of these various streams are all in communion with each other, and the remaining 25% broadly similar again I felt justified in treating this as one group. Next largest are the reasonably well-defined Anglican (110 million), Baptist (105 million) and Lutheran (90 million) churches. Six down, five to go.

Next, we can coalesce all the Calvinist churches into one group, again based not on central hierarchy but of doctrine, style and practice. This includes all those that would call themselves Presbyterian, Reformed or Congregational, of which there are 80 million. Then comes 80 million Methodists again reasonably self-contained. Now it gets harder. The next largest self-contained group is those who are called the Oriental Orthodox (62 million). This is quite separate from the Eastern Orthodox and includes the Coptic, Syriac and Armenian churches over 90% of whom are in communion with each other. Having pulled together nine defendable groups that leaves 200 million made up of a very long tail of diverse confessions. Maintaining the plan of finding the next two largest groups I discovered two huge groupings that I previously did not know existed. It was very humbling to find the 60 million believers who were part of a dozen or so national churches affiliated into the African-Initiated Church (AIC). The origins of this lies within the anti-colonial movements of the nineteenth century. The vast majority of their member congregations are unsurprisingly in Africa. That left room for one more well-defined group from the remaining 140 million.

Let me point out that the thousands of remaining stand-alone churches that remain in the 'Miscellaneous group' contains Quakers, Brethren, Amish, Anabaptists, Moravians and Messianic Judaism. But to maintain my self-imposed rule of lifting the next largest contiguous group I then discovered the 25 million-strong state church of China or, as it is known, the Three-Self Patriotic Movement. Hence the eleven largest contiguous groups of churches are as follows:

Catholic	1,329,000,000
Pentecostal	280,000,000
Eastern Orthodox	220,000,000
Anglican	110,000,000
Baptist	105,000,000
Lutheran	90,000,000
Reformed/Calvinist	80,000,000
Methodist	80,000,000
Oriental Orthodox	62,000,000
African Indigenous Church	60,000,000
Three-Self Patriotic Movement	25,000,000
Other & Unaffiliated	114,000,000
	2,555,000,000

I stress that this was largely just for my own curiosity. However, having completed the listing exercise, when I reflected on what it had produced, I couldn't help but feel somewhat dissatisfied. Not only because there were groups listed of which I had no personal knowledge nor affinity toward, but also because I ended up with a huge and diverse miscellaneous group which didn't feel right at all. In short – this attempt failed to identify 12 church tribes. So, I decided to have another stab at it.

Tribes based on schism

This time I would not separate the tribes based on head count. Besides, we can see in the censuses of the nation of Israel conducted in the book of Numbers[1] that the tribes were all very different sizes. So, ignoring current size I decided to look at the various fracture points that the Church has endured over the last two millennia to see if that would produce a more satisfying notional twelve tribes. Perhaps by looking at the point of schism we may find a unifying principle.

First some self-imposed ground rules. I decided to progress through history and identify any schism that produced a significant separate movement that I considered remained Christian (purely my opinion but I needed to exclude the thousands of heretics) and secondly that they were still in existence today. The basic timeline is well documented and if you wanted to attempt it yourself, within two minutes on the internet you will have caught me up.

That being said, the very first major Church split isn't usually printed on the Church timeline. The first fracture point was when the Church abandoned it Jewish roots at Nicaea (AD 325) leaving what we now call the Jewish Messianic Church, which is still active and growing today, albeit in relatively small numbers.

The next two significant splits came at the Councils of Ephesus (431) and Chalcedon (451) where a common definition of the divine and human natures of Christ were agreed. This led first to the break-away of the Assyrian Church at Ephesus and then, at Chalcedon, The Oriental Orthodox and Coptic Church. Next, we hit the Great Schism of 1054 which separated what we call the Eastern Orthodox Church from rest of the Catholic Church.

That takes us nicely to the mid-16th century from which point a series of consequential Church divisions began with The

---

[1] Census 1 is documented in the book of Numbers chapter 1; Census 2 in chapter 26

Reformation of 1517 when we gained the Lutheran Church. In 1534 Henry VIII sows the seeds of the Anglican Communion which takes shape over the next fifty years during which period we see the birth of the Calvinist or Reformed confession from around 1536. In 1609 John Smyth started the Baptist movement and then in 1650 and 1738 respectively we see the Quaker and Methodist movements break out from within the Anglican Church. Then in the early 20th century we see the Pentecostal awakening.

I've lost count. Let's tot them up. That is Jewish Messianic, Assyrian, Oriental Orthodox, Eastern Orthodox, Lutheran, Anglican, Calvinist, Baptist, Quaker, Methodist and then Pentecostal. That comes to eleven. Wow, we got to that number quite easily. But then it hit me. I was looking at this from a largely Protestant retrospective viewpoint. What about historic splits within the Coptic, Orthodox or Catholic churches? I will need to wind the clock back and add in some of their sub-denominations.

Let's look at the Catholic Church first which post-Luther has managed to fully reconnect with two former breakaways. Firstly, the Eastern Catholic Church which split from the Assyrian Church in 1552 and is now in full communion with Rome. A less well documented split was that of the Maronites in Lebanon who, after years of persecution, in 684 appointed their own patriarch. This act was opposed by Rome – a situation that lasted until 1736.

Reforms to the Eastern Orthodox Church produced the separation of a major group that held on to the former rites, and which therefore became known as the Old Believers. These are mainly in Russia. (I know a lot of old believers, but none of them Russian!) Russia has been the seedbed to a more wholesale potential separation of the Russian Orthodox Church from the rest of the Eastern Orthodox Church which has been gathering traction since 1971.

The Oriental Orthodox Church has largely allowed internal divisions to develop into full schism favouring a somewhat loose pragmatic structure to keep them all within communion, which now can appear almost incomprehensible to outsiders, such as me. As already mentioned, the Assyrian Church, which is also known as the Church of the East, had a major split in 1552 whereby a large proportion returned to communion with Rome. The rest continued as one entity until 1974 when a group known as the Ancient Church of the East broke away.

I guess there are few evangelicals with any knowledge of the Lebanese Maronites or the Ancient Church of the East. I certainly hadn't. But neither my ignorance of them nor my geographical or cultural distance from them gives me any right to dismiss the soundness of their faith.

So where does that take us. I had eleven groups in the well documented protestant timeline. If I now add The Old Believers, and the Ancient Church of the East that takes me to thirteen. Perhaps I should stop there. It doesn't appear that this methodology has produced a more satisfying result. I know it was driven out of my own curiosity, but I had hoped for better.

Well, so much for my attempts at defining twelve notional tribes based on denominations; an exercise which on reflection was pretty much a waste of time. So why have I wasted your time in making you read it? (I did give you the chance to opt out!) I decided to keep it in, principally because this is the logical starting point anyone would have to work through to then come to the realisation that such an arbitrary exercise was flawed.

Perhaps looking at denominations isn't the right place to find church-tribes. It was at this point I had an idea.

The Tribes of Israel – revisited.

Welcome back to those who skipped forward – you didn't miss much.

Returning to the Old Testament and the twelve tribes of Israel, I was curious to understand more about the differences between each tribe and whether we could see any parallels with our present-day One Church. Perhaps this might help us detect twelve church-tribes?

What I wanted to know is what each of the tribes of Israel were like. It is easy to define them by geography, nearly every Bible has that map at the rear, but I wanted to know what motivated them, what their priorities were, what really mattered to them. That was much harder to define but there are a few useful places to look:

Firstly, in the names given to each of the tribal patriarchs. If you aren't aware, they are, in birth order: Reuben, Simeon, Levi, Judah, Dan, Naphtali, Gad, Asher, Issachar, Zebulun, Joseph and Benjamin. The more observant will note that whilst these are the sons of Israel the names of the tribes differed slightly. Levi was not allotted an inheritance and the two sons of Joseph, Manasseh and Ephraim, are each considered tribes[1] thus giving Joseph a double inheritance. These names are listed in Genesis chapter 35 verses 22b to 26a. These names all carry meaning in the original Hebrew.

The second and third places we can look, as already mentioned, are the blessings that Jacob gave in Genesis 49, and those given by Moses in Deuteronomy chapter 33.

Finally, we can look at the lives of the twelve sons to see how they behaved. Perhaps by distilling the meanings of the names, the blessings (some of which were more like warnings) and their lifestyles, we might be able to identify the ethos of each one.

That's the plan, to consider the twelve tribes of Israel and see how they may be reflected in today's Church and in so doing this may identify twelve hypothetical Church-tribes.

---

[1] Technically they were half-tribes.

I am indebted to the work of Rabbi Simon Jackson[1] for his work on the subject of tribal identities which I have repurposed into the context of twelve hypothetical Church-tribes, and added some of my own observations. Each Church-tribe is based on a tribe of Israel, but I am not going to use the original tribal names but a version of Rabbi Jackson's descriptors. They are, however, listed in the usual birth order, so if you need to cross-refence you can. And please remember, this is just an experiment which we shall reflect upon once we have completed it.

The Twelve *Hypothetical* Church-Tribes

1 – The Caring Tribe

They speak up for and defend the vulnerable and are the first to offer shelter to the oppressed. They have a strong sense of responsibility not only to the defenceless but also for the other churches. Their numbers are large, and its history is long, which means they carry some guilt from the past which may hold them back. However, they have boundless energy, and with this energy comes a degree of instability. If harnessed properly they will bring refreshing and cleansing to many, but if unchanneled they may have a tendency to both overpower and erode others.

2 – The Defender Tribe

They are fearless and unashamedly filled with a righteous anger, ready to oppose those who speak falsehood. They find it almost impossible to compromise, even at their own expense. Inevitably they sometimes speak without consideration of the implications, not willing to play political games. Some churches think that they sometimes go too far. They are particularly close to The Serving Tribe but distance themselves from some of the other tribes.

[1] 'Twelve Tribes – Twelve Paths' by Rabbi Simon Jackson, published on chabad.org

3 – The Serving Tribe

They dedicate their lives to serving, being adept in practical ways and happy to serve others. They are committed to what they see as a higher calling, often at the expense of family and other close relationships. They delight in study and are born worshippers. They are free from concerns of the material world, even to the extent of going off-grid.

4 – The Pioneering Tribe

They are always the first into new things and other churches acknowledge their leadership. They are entirely comfortable with that position, dealing fairly and equitably with others. They are readily able to take on the selfless attitude that this requires. They do not seek help from others and will expect to have the upper hand when confronted.

5 – The Breakout Tribe

They have great strength and will not be confined by the expectations or pre-imposed limitations of others. They have great wisdom and are readily able to ensure that even the smallest of actions will deliver a proportionally huge impact. They have had to deal with complex emotions, sometimes feeling like the black sheep of the churches, which has sown a degree of inherent discontent.

6- The Free-Spirited Tribe

They hate the status quo and are only really happy when they are breaking new ground. Fiercely independent, they have to take care not to 'speak words of beauty' just to please others. Abounding in God's favour and blessing.

7 – The Warrior Tribe

They are always ready to fight for their beliefs, to defend their cherished values and protect freedom. They will therefore be happy with the best portion. They are unphased by politics and can use it adeptly. Some may consider them to be lucky, but they know they are blessed.

8 – The Prosperous Tribe

They are blessed with material resources beyond the norm and have more than what is necessary for survival. Not only that, but they also know how to enjoy it. They are strong and able to defend their faith. They are happy but sometimes seen as impetuous and wasteful.

9 – The Scholarly Tribe

They immerse themselves with great dedication to study, which inevitably brings them great joy and contentment. They are able to complete the mission given them and will build a foundation based on wisdom, clarity and direction. They are known as those who know what ought to be done and as such are often seen in the vanguard of new things.

10 – The Marketplace Tribe

They flow freely into the marketplace to redeem the treasures within the material world. They are trusted by outsiders. They are brave risktakers, always ready to answer the call, including when it means new, entrepreneurial challenges. They have a close relationship with The Scholarly Tribe.

11 – The Thriving Tribe

They know adversity and not only survive it but thrive from it, achieving greatness through such challenges. Despite a hostile environment, they maintain their integrity. The powerful light that emerges from them has two dimensions: the ability to not forget their spiritual roots; and to be fruitful amongst their afflictions. A place of refreshing. Choicest of blessings, fruitful, favourer. Their reputation will affect nations.

12 – The Haven Tribe

The haven for God-lovers who find sanctuary within. They are hungry for God, and passionately seek Him out to devour, consume and worship. They are clever and crafty, able to wrongfoot the enemy although this can sometimes make them appear quarrelsome. They know what it is like to go through tough times as well as good times, when they delight to share the spoils with others. They are fiercely loyal, especially to The Thriving Tribe with whom they are particularly close.

Well, what has that given us? Certainly, a new take on the tribes that may potentially make up the One Church.

Then it hit me. Tribal identity was never going to be about the denominations; it is a description of the smaller groups that naturally form <u>within</u> congregations, and what is even more pleasing, <u>across</u> congregations. It is about the way we each fit within the One Church with our unique character and gifting.

Let's put that idea to the test. And you can help me.

Testing the Tribes

Firstly, I want you to consider your particular part of the One Church. You can define that however you wish. It may be the congregation you meet with each Sunday, but more likely a smaller group that you spend time amongst, or if you prefer a parachurch organisation you are linked with (more on those later). How you define it is up to you but having made your selection, ask yourself this question:

"Does this group represent my <u>primary</u> <u>identity</u> as a member of the Church? Or in other words is the group you thought of <u>your</u> <u>tribe</u>?"

193

If the answer is no, you need to make a new selection. You need to identify the group of believers that <u>you belong to</u>, that shares your heart. This may be different to whose parochial list you appear upon. It may not be a congregation at all, it may not even be a defined group, but find the group that best describes <u>your</u> tribe.

Done that? Good.

What I suspect is that most people will identify with a group much smaller than the congregation they regularly attend. I also suspect that the many will include people who are not even part of their congregation but with whom they are in regular relationship.

Once you have that group in your mind, the next thing is to go through the list of twelve hypothetical Church-Tribes listed previously and see if one of them jumps out at you. I have no idea if this will work. But I am so excited to find out. I can't comment on your findings – because they are yours! But thank you for playing.

<u>Inter-Congregational Smudge</u>

A couple of real-life observations.

I am an unashamedly middle-aged Christian man, and have been in the local church-scene (a strange phrase but you know what I mean) for over four decades. Recently, I decided to make a list of my ten closest male Christian friends. Perhaps you should do the same (although list female friends if you are a lady). In composing my list, I excluded anyone who was a relative but included those who were not currently regularly attending any congregation. I didn't limit it to those who were still local to me, or indeed those with whom I have managed to maintain contact over the years (a common male failing I fear). Go on, make your own list and we will see if you have the same realisation as I had.

Have you done it? No? Oh well, you are clearly free-spirited and who am I to tell you what to do.

The first thing I found was that after I had written down the first six names I began to dry up. Perhaps that is just me. I got to ten names soon enough though. I then sat back and noticed how many congregations were represented by these ten people. The answer – eight. To be fair, several had moved away, but nonetheless my ten closest same-sex Christian friends attend eight different congregations. At no point have I ever considered that they are no longer my friends because we attend a different service each week. And that is just personal friendship. How much more so if we consider those with whom we share a deep spiritual destiny, our tribe. There is a deep truth in the fact that our personal networks extend beyond our congregations. We should stop ignoring it, or making excuses for it, and fully embrace this wonderful inter-congregational smudge.

I was giving someone a lift home the other day as they returned from a Saturday prayer and worship event that they had attended alongside a dozen or so others from a variety of congregations. She is a prayer warrior and for quite some time had been part of this group which met online weekly to pray, but this Saturday event was the first in-person gathering. As we drove, she commented on how good the day had been and then made a remark that I think demonstrates the idea of Church-Tribes we are considering. And what is more, it is probably a comment you could hear in thousands of churches every week.

In describing her appreciation and the satisfaction she had for the day of free-flowing prayer and worship she had just participated in, she described it as the place she felt at home. But what struck me more was the comparison she then made with her congregation. She described how, having been appointed by her pastor as the prayer leader in her congregation, she was continually frustrated at how hard it was to get more than a light dusting of people to attend the weekly prayer meeting. She was the same person in each prayer meeting – the online one and her local congregational one. She exercised the same gifts, she was filled with the same Holy Spirit, but only one of these meetings felt like, as she put it, her tribe.

Does this mean she is in the wrong congregation? I don't think that necessarily follows. Besides, the online prayer group patently isn't a congregation. It is, however, part of the One Church!

On reflection, observations such as these I think may demonstrate that the hypothetical Church-Tribes I listed earlier are meant to exist **between congregations**. Do you remember when we were talking about the Church as a body, we commented on the fact that the circulatory, nervous and lymphatic systems work across every member. Have we stumbled over the fact that Church-Tribes, or to put it simply 'the personal network relationships that we naturally gravitate toward', are such a bodily system? Is this the very glue that is meant to hold the One Church together? If it is, then I think we have made a very important discovery. If we understand our own source of identity and security, then we will be in a better place to actively show the love and grace to those whose different beliefs and practices threaten to deter us.

And what is more, these tribal micro-groups may well form the backbone of our end-times Church.

18. Leadership within the One Church

If we accept there is just One Church, not just in theory but in realised actuality, and that such a One Church comprises an amorphous mass of individuals, congregations and denominations, then it raises a question of how could it ever act as one entity? This is a question of leadership.

The Three Governance Models

Today it is broadly true that every denomination has adopted one of three generic leadership structures. I am not talking about the leadership of each congregation – that is the subject for another book – but I am considering how the entire denomination is structured. In particular I want to focus on the relationship between each congregation and the... well, let's call it The Centre. By that I mean the institution(s) that define the denomination as a distinct entity. The Centre may encompass people, offices, funding, synods, publications, websites, laws, rites or a much looser notion of shared mission or identity. Perceptions therefore of The Centre may range from The Denominational Hierarchy or simply The Wider Network. Whatever it is called there are only three ways that a member congregation can interact with The Centre.

Firstly, there is the belief that there is no centre and that each congregation is itself entirely and completely independent. The leaders of that congregation would be appointed from within with no reference to any outside body. This type of structure, if we can call it such, we call **Congregationalist.** A historic term that is not a statement of doctrine – only one of structure.

The other two descriptors define the situation when there is a centre and differ only by the direction of the authority flow. In simple terms, Top Down or Bottom Up.

If the leader of a congregation is, in its broadest term, appointed by the denomination and as such is answerable to a representative of The Centre, then we call this structure **Episcopal** from the Greek word Episkopos, usually translated as bishop or overseer. I understand that in most cases the congregation will have a say in agreeing to the person who has been nominated to lead them, but nevertheless the direction of travel is top down. As the leader has been appointed from The Centre then that is where they are accountable. You could say 'The bishop is the boss.'

The opposite structure is where the leaders of a congregation are appointed from within (as in Congregationalist) but then someone is nominated to represent them in The Centre. These we call **Presbyterian** where The Centre is made up of representatives, each appointed (usually elected) by their congregations, and working together as equals. Hence, they are answerable to their own congregations and not The Centre, i.e. 'The congregation is the boss.'

If you are in doubt as to whether a specific denomination is Episcopal or Presbyterian a rule-of-thumb is to ask who pays the leaders' wages, or stipend. If they are paid, whether in full or in part, from a central fund then they are most likely Episcopal.

Regardless of which structure is in place we know that God will bring blessing and growth to all of those who are wholly committed to Him. Consequently, I am making no comment on these models of church governance, I can see that God is more than capable of working His purposes through whichever structure is in place.

<u>Inter-Congregational Leadership</u>

That being said, when it comes to inter-congregational co-operation, the type of governance suddenly becomes very important. It will be impossible to expect that members of one denomination would be in any way 'under' the leadership of another. To do so would violate the very nature of those believers' identity. They have chosen their place in the One Church, they are part of that denomination for a reason. To be 'ruled' by another with a different ethos, priorities and style would be entirely incompatible. Such use (or misuse) of authority has been the precise cause of several historical church schisms.

I suspect that most would be comfortable with a degree of inter-denominational co-operation or mission. However, if we are to act as One Church, then perhaps we need to look deeper at God's preferred governance model and how, as diverse entities, we are able to act as one when we need to. In so doing we will see that there is a Biblical model that will allow us to act together, demonstrating our active unity, without compromising our identity.

A couple of chapters ago we explored the idea that the structure of the Church may parallel the Biblical nation of Israel – a nation that contains several tribes that, whilst being distinct, are inter-dependent; a nation that would worship and, when needed, fight as one.

The nation of Israel, when originally established, had no central ruler, no king, no elected president. In fact, when the nation requested that Samuel *"Make us a king to judge us like all the nations,"* [1] we read that God was disappointed with them, saying, *"they have rejected Me, that I should not reign over them."* [2]

By this, we could realistically infer that central governance was not God's preferred model for His nation. If so, does that mean that it is also not His preferred model for church governance? If this were to be the case, then the vast majority of today's Church (specifically 1.8bn of the 2.5bn Christians globally) belong to denominations without such governance. But let's not get too dramatic. I did make the comment way back in an early chapter that centralisation will probably not survive into the end-

---

[1] 1 Samuel 8 v 5
[2] 1 Samuel 8 v 7

times and does have, I believe, some in-built risks when it comes to deception. But for now, in the main, these denominations are functioning perfectly well, and I am not saying there is anything fundamentally wrong with church governance being structured around a central leader(s). Besides, if we continue in First Samuel, we see that when the nation of Israel clamoured to have a king, despite it clearly not being God's preference, He granted their wish, giving rise to what is probably the most important dynastic era in the nation's history – David and Solomon, kings that God showered with success and blessing beyond measure.

But first, let's rewind and look at how God initially brought leadership into his multi-tribal nation.

The Shofet

We find this rather unique governance model in the Book of Judges. The first thing we discover is that God would raise up an individual or individuals to meet an immediate pressing need, usually the need to defend against an aggressor or oppressor. The Hebrew term used to describe this role was *shofet*, which is translated into English as 'judge.' It is closer in meaning to a military leader or deliverer rather than a magistrate. Perhaps the seventh book of the Bible should be called the 'Book of Deliverers'.

The call of God on that individual Deliverer's life was clear and unambiguous and most importantly recognised by all. They were equipped with the skills, but more importantly the faith in God, to see-off the attack.

From One Tribe but Defending the Nation

The next thing we discover when studying the lives of the Biblical Judges is the fact that they came from many, though not all, of the tribes. This was largely because the external threat was targeted in a local area and hence their tribe was best placed to offer the defence. But be clear, that defence was always in the name of the nation of Israel, not the tribe alone, as is evidenced from the following table.

Judge	Tribe	Call to the Nation of Israel (Judges except where stated)
Othniel	Judah	*'The Lord raised up a deliverer for the **children of Israel**.'* 3v9
Ehud	Benjamin	*'When the **children of Israel** cried out... the Lord raised up a deliverer for them.'* 3v15
Shamgar	Unknown	*'He also delivered **Israel**.'* 3v31
Deborah	Ephraim	*'Deborah... was judging **Israel** at that time.'* 4v4
Gideon	Manasseh	*'You shall save **Israel** from the hand of the Midianites.'* 6v14
Tola	Issachar	*'There arose to save **Israel**, Tola.'* 10v1
Jair	Gilead-Manasseh	*'He judged **Israel** twenty-two years.'* 10v3
Jephthah	Gilead-Manasseh	*'Jephthah judged **Israel** six years.'* 12v7
Ibzan	Judah	*'Ibzan of Bethlehem judged **Israel**.'* 12v8
Elon	Zebulun	*'He judged **Israel** ten years.'* 12v11
Abdon	Ephraim	*'He judged **Israel** eight years.'* 12v14
Samson	Dan	*'And he judged **Israel** twenty years in the days of the Philistines.'* 15v20
Samuel	Levi	*'The **children of Israel** said to Samuel, "Do not cease to cry out to the Lord our God for us, that He may save us from the...Philistines"'* 1 Sam 7v8

In passing, we can also see that some of the Judges were considerably more notable than others. Samson gets four chapters, Gideon over three whereas Tola and Elon each get just two verses.

I hope you are getting the idea. In the Book of Judges we see that in times of oppression God raised up a man, or woman, or a couple, to take on the attacks of the day. Some were localised but their call was to the whole nation not their own tribe.

If we were to spend time looking deeper into the lives of the Judges, we would find that few were existing leaders, and many were flawed individuals who wrestled with insecurity, anxiety, temptation and prejudice. They each exhibited different talents and gifts, but all put their faith in God as they stepped (some reluctantly) into the national role. We would also read that in the absence of a Judge the nation slid into compromise with disastrous effect.

This principle has not just been evidenced in a period of roughly four hundred years after the conquest of Canaan, but God has been doing the same ever since. And just like the Judges, it is rarely, if ever, through the established hierarchy of the Church. Let me present a couple examples from history.

<u>Erasmus of Rotterdam</u>

Let me introduce you to a Deliverer that God raised up way back in the middle-ages; someone so important that scholars considering him to be the father of the Reformation despite the fact that he never left the Roman Catholic Church. Someone who transformed access to the Bible across the whole of the known world. And yet few have even heard of his name. Indeed, as my book 'Ancient & Modern: The Search' focused on the people who established new church denominations he didn't even get a mention. His name, Erasmus of Rotterdam (1466-1536). In his day, it is pretty safe to say the Church was riddled with corruption and spiritually dead. Erasmus believed it could be reformed by a return to its Biblical roots. His radical counterculture philosophy was that he believed, "The most exalted aim... will be to obtain a knowledge of the pure and simple Christianity of the Bible."[1] This led him to set about producing a revised translation of the New Testament into Greek and Latin as an alternative to the exclusively used Vulgate version. In doing so he removed several key passages that were never in the original text, but upon which several church

---

[1] From *Ad Servatium,* as quoted by Jean D'Aubigne, *History of the Reformation of the Sixteenth Century*, volume 1. New York: Robert Carter & Brothers, 1853, 124)

practices relied. Such a radical translation could only happen from within the established Church. If he had broken away the translation would have been quashed and never seen the light of day. Instead, he did it with Papal blessing, allowing him to continue and produce several more publications. The importance of Erasmus's translation cannot be overstated. It would not be inaccurate to say that it led directly to the reformations instigated by Martin Luther, Ulrich Zwingli, John Calvin, and the rather more confused English Reformation, all of which do get a mention in my book!

When Luther nailed his 95 theses to the door of the church in Wittenberg on October 31, 1517, the first few were based on Erasmus' translation of repentance in Matthew 3:2. Zwingli's journey to reformation began when he abandoned praying to saints as a direct result of the translation. It also spawned vernacular translations into all seven of the main European languages of the day. Many know that William Tyndale produced the first English translation, an achievement for which he was martyred. Many also know the famous speech he gave as part of his defence to the religious authorities; "If God spare my life, ere many years I will cause a boy that driveth the plow shall know more of the scripture than thou doest." What few people realise is that this oft-quoted statement was actually a paraphrase from Erasmus. Despite Tynedale's untimely death, by 1547 a copy of his translation had been placed in every church in England.

Erasmus is an example of someone whom God raised up to complete a specific task, at a specific time, in a specific place, from within a specific denomination. He wasn't the leader, just the man for the mission. Today, we can quite rightly celebrate the life of this this life-long Catholic (and I would encourage you to read his story) whether or not we are from that denomination ourselves. Indeed, every Protestant Bible traces its roots back to his faithfulness and courage.

Now let me suggest a very different 'Deliverer'.

God is NOT dead.

I remember being a young Christian in the 1970s. Society was drifting away from God and in particular the 'God is Dead' message was being shouted loudly by the culture of the day as scientific discovery upon scientific discovery threatened to cast doubt on the validity of the Bible, the existence of God and hence the faith of millions of people.

At this point God raised up specific people to help frame the response to society and one in particular, Josh MacDowell, wrote the best-selling "Evidence that Demands a Verdict." This book, amongst others, gave us the vocabulary and arguments to respond to the pseudo-scientific counterculture that was invading the Church and society at the time, and deliver God's truth to the world. I don't have to be from the same denomination as Josh MacDowell in order to benefit from the weapon he placed in my hand. Can you see the Judge principle at work here?

I have deliberately used two very different examples. Both Erasmus and Josh MacDowell are examples of people whom God raised up as a Shofet (Deliverer) to wage war for the defence of His Church. Neither had delegated authority. Both spoke out against the false claims of the day. I am sure you can think of many others.

If this is God's model for cross-tribe leadership we should expect that He will raise up individuals at a specific time, in a specific place, from a specific denomination, from a specific tribe, in order to demonstrate His purposes to a needy world. And when such a person stands up, we should be ready and willing to take our place on the defensive (or offensive) line.

19. Where do parachurch organisations fit?

The final anomaly we ned to consider is those ministries and organisations whose roots do not exist within a specific denomination (or congregation) and which have therefore acquired the unhelpful moniker of 'parachurch' organisations.

First a definition. I don't like to quote from Wikipedia, for obvious reasons, but I think the definition of a parachurch organisation that is listed there works well:

'Parachurch organisations are Christian faith-based organisations that work outside and across denominations to engage in social welfare and evangelism. They seek to come alongside the church and specialise in things that individual churches may not be able to specialise in by themselves.' [1]

I particularly like the idea that a parachurch organisation is a 'specialist' in an area that the rest of the church may not be able to do themselves. Though it isn't stated, I suppose the reason that such an organisation would be able to deliver such a specialism would be the combination of the resources, talent and infrastructure that has allowed them to focus on their particular aspect of the Christian mission or message.

The Wikipedia page then goes on to list some of the more widely known examples under a few rather broad headings. I have recast the categorisation to be, in my opinion, a little more meaningful; added a few more examples from my personal knowledge; and inserted some comments. This is not meant to be an exhaustive list, purely just examples to aid our understanding of what sort of activities are included.

---

[1] https://en.wikipedia.org/wiki/List_of_parachurch_organizations

Examples of Parachurch Organisations

General Evangelism
>   Billy Graham Evangelistic Association, plus, the personal ministry of
>   every other full-time evangelist.

Targeted Evangelism & Discipleship
>   Youth for Christ, Youth with a Mission, Teen Challenge, Boys' Brigade,
>   Prisons Fellowship, City Missions, Intervarsity Christian Fellowship,
>   Cru (formerly Campus Crusade for Christ), Christians in Sport,
>   Athletes in Action, Christian Motorcycle Assoc., Christian Voice for Men
>   Women of Faith, Christians in Science, etc.

International Mission & Relief
>   Christian Missionary Fellowship, Mercy Ships, Open Doors,
>   Operation Mobilisation, Samaritans Purse, Barnabas Fund,
>   Christian Aid, World Vision, Tearfund, CARE, etc.
>   It would appear that most established missionary societies come from
>   within singular denominations, so don't strictly qualify as parachurch
>   by this definition.

Social Welfare, Care and Support
>   YMCA, Christians against Poverty, Street Pastors.

Teaching and Bible
>   Gideons International, The Bible Society, Scripture Union, etc.
>   Wycliffe Bible Translators (and other translators)
>   Christianity Today (plus many other magazines).

Educational, Apologetics & Political
>   Several Bible schools and seminaries, although many have a singular
>   denominational bias.
>   Christian Concern, Christian Research Institute, Theos Thinktank.

Creative & Media
>   Many Christian TV channels and radio stations, The Jesus Film Project
>   Covenant Players, Saltmine Trust, plus every other Christian musician,
>   singer, playwright, actor, director, author, painter, sculptor, etc.

Firstly, let me get the apologies out of the way. This is only meant to be a list of examples, not a definitive list. Some of the organisations shown are well-known, others from personal knowledge which may be out of date. The categorisation is personal and arbitrary so please give me some grace if I have inadvertently caused any offence. My intent was simply to highlight the wide diversity of activities that exist.

Surely this is evidence that, *'The harvest truly is plentiful, '*[1] and those who feel the call of God on their lives to step out into that particular harvest field have done so. The faithful workers and volunteers who heed that call are all to be commended for the great work they do preaching, translating, educating, broadcasting, performing, comforting, feeding, homing and vaccinating regardless of whether their local church is involved in that work or not.

Let's reflect on this imperfect list. Ignoring my initial categorisation based on their activities, let me now re-classify them on the <u>motivation</u> that drives them. In so doing we see some quite different groups emerge:

Evangelists: Those driven to share the gospel in a wide diversity of harvest fields,

Missionaries: Those able to establish new and lasting Christian work in areas both home and overseas,

Guardians: Those compelled to offer compassion, protection, support and relief both home and overseas,

Bible-Lovers: Those driven to get the word of God to those who need to hear it, and to make disciples who live by it,

Communicators: Those able to speak deep into people's hearts through a story, a song, a picture or a well-structured argument.

---

[1] Matthew 9 v 37

Again, this is not a perfect list but bear with me – I will return to it in a few pages.

Goodbye Parachurch

Having listed some of the organisations that we might consider as being parachurch, let us now look at the word: 'parachurch'.

The prefix para- come from the Greek where it usually has the meaning of *'At or to one side of, besides, or side-by-side.'* [1]

Although it can also mean 'abnormal or defective' (as in paranormal or paranoid), let's assume a parachurch organisation isn't meant to be a defective one!

So, a parachurch organisation is one that is positioned 'beside' church. This can only be the case if by 'church' we mean a local congregation. If we accept God's decree that there is but One Church, then linguistically we have to place any parachurch organisation outside of that One Church. This is clearly unworkable.

It is funny, but I have noticed that when I hear anyone use the word parachurch they invariably add the caveat that they "Don't like the term." Well of course they don't, it is lexicographically meaningless.

However, the ministries classified as 'parachurch' are anything but meaningless. They are as much a part of the One Church as the Sunday service. As we saw in a previous chapter from the Apostle Paul's greetings (his Who's Who messages) he includes several individuals that we would today term parachurch ministers, and foremost amongst these we would have to include Paul himself.

---

[1] https://www.wordreference.com/definition/para-

So, it is time to bid a fond farewell to the word parachurch. It has served us inadequately for many years, but it is time to say our goodbyes. Please join me at the graveside, bow your head in silence as we gently lower these ten letters into the earth. Ashes to ashes, dust to dust, in sure and certain hope of their resurrection into more useful words such as Hurrah!

But what word should we use to describe these ministries? I am quite taken with the one Wikipedia used, namely **Specialists.** Let's try that for now and see how it works.

If we are to accept that such Specialist Ministries are not 'to one side of' but rather are a core part of the One Church, how does this work when they are not part of any denominational structure and their activities are, in the main, independent of ecclesiastical oversight. Does that not by definition place them on the outside? We have a conundrum and once again we can look to Church history to help us chart a path through it and provide us with the vocabulary that may help to include these Specialist Ministries, together with the thousands I didn't list, squarely within the One Church model.

The Apostolic Church

Starting in New Testament times, we have seen plenty of ministers operating outside of the local church structure. Chief amongst these were the Apostles, or to use the Latin translation of the same word, the Missionaries. This ministry fitted well within the One Church at the time and there was no conflict. The Apostle Paul was clearly operating outside of the local church structure or, as Ralph D Winter puts it, "Paul was <u>sent off</u> not <u>sent out</u> by the Antioch congregation. He may have reported back to it, but did not take orders from it."[1]

---

[1] "History of the Parachurch." by Ralph D Winter 1973. WSN Press, 100 Lake Hart Drive--2500, Orlando, FL 32832.

Studying the writing of the early Church fathers we see a duality of structures with the early Church. On the one hand we have a strong and established local church structure overseen by a leader (the Episkopos) and run by elders (the Presbyters). On the other hand, we cannot deny that there are others operating beyond this structure. Evidence shows us that the Apostles were part of the Church but that they did not fit within the local church structure. So how did they fit in? Were they in ultimate charge? Were the leaders of the churches that Paul established answerable to Paul as some sort of apostolic pontifex? It would appear not. As we have seen, he described himself as merely *'him who plants'*[1] and not him who rules. Yes, he freely gave correction and instruction but never claimed 'ownership' of his planted churches. Even when they were drifting into error he never returned to, for example, replace the leadership as tempting it may have been, especially in Corinth. His work was done – he was an Apostle, a Missionary, a planter. The overseers were left to oversee.

Church in the Middle Ages

Winding the clock forward from New Testament times we arrive in the medieval period where, as we have seen, there were only a handful of different denominations in existence. We'll focus on Western Europe, which was dominated (correct term) by what we now call the Roman Catholic Church, an organisation with a rigid structure of provinces, dioceses and parishes. But have you ever considered that even within this somewhat autocratic organisational structure there were several thriving Specialist Ministries operating beside the local churches, and that the established structure had no authority over them? What's more, it was these organisations that were largely responsible for the growth of the Church, for the provision of care to the needy, for the maintenance of access to the scriptures, for the development of doctrine, and for the survival of the very existence of the Church in the periods when the Church had been all but wiped-out.

---

[1] 1 Corinthians 3 v 7

These organisations were so important to the life of the Church that the father of the Reformation, Martin Luther, considered that they alone held the life of the Church – not the stale and corrupt local church structure. What were these organisations? If you haven't guessed already, I am talking of the monastic orders. Structurally a local bishop had no authority over the head of a monastic institution, usually termed the abbot. There was, of course, occasional friction but in the main both co-existed side-by-side (i.e. para-).

Let me introduce you to a couple of terms that have been used to describe the differences between these two aspects of the mediaeval Church. The local church was made up of all the people within its congregation without regard to gender, race or class. Whereas the monastic order was made up of a subset, usually defined by gender and often described by the somewhat gender specific 'Brotherhood'.

And please don't overlook the fact the Martin Luther was himself an Augustinian monk. It is easy to dismiss monks and nuns as just part of the pre-Reformation Church but let's not throw the baby out with the bathwater. Most of these organisations remain in existence to this day and continue with their ongoing good work.

I hope you can see that in the middle ages the same principle existed that we saw in the apostolic era. There is a local church structure and a cross-church structure, the latter being focussed on different, often specific needs of the day.

Early Eighteenth Century

One of the most enlightening discoveries I made in researching for the book Ancient & Modern: The Search was the widely reported activity of prophets that spoke on the streets of London (and other cities) in the early years of the eighteenth century. This movement became known as The French Prophets and was widely reported in the press as a message from God to the nation. The verifiable evidence of the operation of the prophetic gift (as well as other instances of healings and miracles) shattered my assumption that the gifts of the Holy Spirit re-entered the Church in the Pentecostal movement of the early twentieth century.

For brevity I won't go into the details of The French Prophets, but they are another historical example of a Specialist Ministry operating 'beside' or more accurately in their case 'opposing' the established religious order of the day, not dissimilar to how the Biblical prophets often did.

Early Nineteenth Century

Moving further forward we arrive at the great evangelistic and missionary era of the early nineteenth century. In this period, a great revival was born, led by evangelists such as John Wesley, George Whitefield and Jonathan Edwards, and new churches were established by missionaries such as William Carey and David Livingston (to name but two).

John Wesley was very clear at the outset of his ministry that his work was 'beside' the established Church and forbade any of his converts to leave their local Anglican congregation. This continued until such time as he had to ordain his own ministers at which point the Methodist movement, for which he is now known, was born.

Local and Specialist

So, there is plenty of historical evidence of there being a duality of structure in practice, **one local <u>and</u> one specialist**. But is there a Biblical rationale for how these ministries are to fit within the One Church? I believe there may be, but I must warn you that what I am about to say may be a little controversial. I might be wrong, but I think the idea has solid merit. You decide for yourself. Ready? Okay, here goes.

When writing to the church at Ephesus, a thriving church with an established structure, Paul stated that there were 'other' ministries that Christ had personally provided to the Church for the purpose of *'the equipping of the saints.'*[1] Specifically, he went on to list these: *'Some as apostles, some prophets, some evangelists, and some pastors and teachers'*[2]

Ask yourself the question, why would he list these ministries to an already established and thriving Church? Could it be that the so called five-fold ministries were in fact all Specialist Ministries and were therefore already freely operating outside of the established local church structure which was focussed on the needs of the local community? Let's take a closer look.

Whilst it is reasonably easy to accept that both an evangelist and an apostle (or missionary) could be considered to be operating outside of the local church, it is more challenging to consider if a prophet or teacher would be, let alone a pastor. Surely a pastor (or shepherd) is an alternative term for a church leader. Hold that thought – let's deal with teacher and prophet first.

One of the most important non-Biblical writings that we have, from the early church period is the first-century manuscript known as 'The Lord's Teaching Through the Twelve Apostles to the Nations' or as it is more commonly termed 'The Didache'. Whilst this is not the inspired Word of God, it does (together with other contemporary writings) nonetheless give us a valuable insight as to how the Church really operated during the apostolic era. In it we see that each church (which of course existed largely underground due to periodic persecution) should expect to be visited by travelling teachers and prophets who would come to deliver Godly instruction or a specific prophetic message. The local congregation, being duly tasked, would weigh such input gravely

---

[1] Ephesians 4 v 12
[2] Ephesians 4 v 11

213

before accepting it.[1] Both prophets and teachers were itinerant ministries in the early Church, interacting with any church that would value and accept their input. Ask yourself where does your Bible teaching come from? Is it exclusively from within your local congregation, or is it not from books, conferences, podcasts, TV & radio messages, blogs, articles or social media? Teachers as well as prophets clearly operate as a Specialist Ministry today.

There is little doubt that we saw apostles, evangelists, teachers and prophets all operating as Specialist Ministries in the Apostolic era – and in describing the work of the monastic orders in the Middle Ages when I said that,

"It was these organisations that were largely responsible for the growth of the Church, for the provision of care to the needy, for the maintenance of access to the scriptures, for the development of doctrine, and for the survival of the very existence of the Church in the periods when the Church had been all but wiped-out."

You can clearly see the evangelist, apostle and teacher evidenced in these activities. There is little doubt that The French Prophets were in fact prophets, and when I described Wesley, Whitefield, Edwards, Carey and Livingston as evangelists and missionaries (or apostles) you wouldn't have batted an eyelid.

But pastors? I admit that on first inspection this appears a little harder to digest, but let me assure you, a pastor is expressly meant to be a Specialist Ministry with a vitally important role to fulfil across denominations and congregations.

Specialist Pastors?

Firstly, lets dispel the myth that pastor simply means church leader. This usage originates from the reformers Calvin and Zwingli who introduced the term pastor to replace the Catholic

---

[1] Didache 11 v 1 to 13 v 18

term 'priest' in the minds of their post-Reformation followers. Prior to 1517 the term pastor was not used at all in the context of congregational leadership.

The Greek word translated as pastor in the list of so-called five-fold ministries[1] is used 18 other times in the New Testament. It is translated as 'shepherd' in <u>every</u> <u>other</u> verse. Hence, we can use pastor and shepherd interchangeably, and even with my limited knowledge of farming I am confident in saying that a shepherd is not the chief sheep. Pastor does not mean church leader. As already stated, we have the presbyter (elder) for that role.

Armed with the knowledge that pastor means shepherd, we can now look into the Old Testament and discover that most of the national leaders of Israel were either literally or figuratively shepherds, namely: Abraham[2], Isaac[3], Joseph[4], Moses[5], Joshua[6], and David[7]. It is interesting to note that none of these leaders owned the flocks they tended, a minor fact which underpins that the pastor does not mean the owner or leader of the flock.

The role of the shepherd was quite simply to *'watch over their sheep.'*[8] That of course does not mean to just watch idly as their sheep either go hungry or, worse still, are attacked by a predator. Implicit in the *watching* is the taking of the necessary actions to feed and protect.

The shepherd's role over his flock is therefore to <u>watch</u> (the flock, the strays, the food-source, any external threats), then to <u>act</u> (move the flock to safety, pursue the strays, be ruthless with infiltrators and threats.)

---

[1] Ephesians 4 v 11
[2] Genesis 13 v 7
[3] Genesis 30 v 29
[4] Genesis 37 v 2
[5] Exodus 3 v 1
[6] Numbers 27 vs 15-20
[7] Psalm 78 vs 70-72
[8] 1 Peter 5 v 2

The pastor's role within the One Church is exactly the same. They are to **Watch** then **Act**. Jesus, as the Good Shepherd, is the perfect example of how the pastor ministry should operate at its most effective.

What we do need to consider, however, is what happens when the Specialist Ministry called shepherd does not operate within the One Church. Let's heed the clear and severe warnings of the prophets:

'They were scattered because there was no shepherd.' [1]

'For the shepherds have become dull-hearted, and have not sought the Lord ... and all their flocks shall be scattered.' [2]

'My people have been lost sheep, their shepherds have led them astray.' [3]

The absence of a shepherd (or bad shepherding) will result in the flock (i.e. the One Church) being scattered. That is the clear unambiguous message repeated many, many times throughout the scriptures.

We could even say that anything that causes the One Church to fragment is **counter-shepherd** or the result of the failure of the pastoral ministry. Wow! Let that sink in.

The premise of this book is to address the wholesale fragmentation of God's One Church. So does that meant I am now laying the guilt of the thousands of denominations squarely at the doorstep of the shepherds who failed to watch over the Church? I don't mean local church 'pastors' but the national One Church pastors who failed to step up, to watch and to act. Perhaps the guilt does lie there but, as you know, it is not for me to judge.

---

[1] Ezekiel 34 v 5
[2] Jeremiah 10:21
[3] Jeremiah 50:6

To clarify. The Pastor Specialist Ministry is meant to operate outside of the local congregation. This is akin to the Episkopos we read of in the New Testament, but to say that a modern-day bishop (of whichever denomination) fulfils that role does come with handcuffs as they are to watch over the One Church **as a whole** and not just their denomination. Their role is to endorse good sources of (spiritual) food, to warn about heresy, to identify threats, and to pursue the strays. They are to be a bridge-builder between congregations in a way that local leaders could never be. And, of course, each local leader is free to either accept their wisdom or not, because the pastor, just like all five-fold ministers, has zero direct authority over them.

Specialist Ministries

These Specialist Ministries (I think the term is growing on me) do not replace the duties of every Christian believer to operate to some degree in each of those areas. For example, we are all supposed to share our faith, without being an evangelist; to encourage someone from the scriptures without being a teacher; to hear from God and speak prophetically without calling ourself a prophet; to guard over each other without being a pastor.

Finally, let's relook at the list of Specialist Ministries we composed earlier, to see if there is any evidence of them looking anything like the five-fold ministries. Scroll back a few pages to see the terms I used to describe their core motivations I used: evangelists, missionaries, guardians, Bible-lovers and communicators. Admittedly in composing these terms I knew exactly where I was going with this line of thought, but I hope that when you read them at first they didn't grate with you. The evangelists and apostle ministries are of course easy to spot. So too are those helping to make disciples, sharing the word of God, and those able to communicate deep into the heart. Are these not the teacher and prophet ministries? And then there are those whose very existence is for the protection of others. Are these not, to some degree, acting as the pastor ministries?

Perhaps you may find this a stretch too far, and I did say it was controversial, but I believe that considering the five-fold ministries as defining the Specialist Ministries (or what we used to call parachurch organisations) has some merit.

Conclusion: The Manifesto

I am a scientist by training and spent the first years of my working life in a laboratory whilst I gained a degree in chemistry. As part of this training, one of the things I learned was that when a research paper is published in an official journal it must be accompanied by what is known as an abstract. The abstract, which always appears at the beginning, is an overview which gives other researchers a general understanding without them having to read the entire document.

I may have it at the end but I'm now going to provide you with an abstract that summarises the main points present in this book. As you read it see if there is anything that you disagree with.

Abstract

There is only One Church, regardless of what we may observe around us, and we are commanded to love all people, and this includes Christians who hold opposing views whom we need to lovingly accept and fellowship with. When it comes to the difficult issues that seek to divide us, we don't need to change our convictions – but we must not assume that our position is the only right one, just that it is the right one for us. We have no right to condemn others. Seeking unity by attempting to find a common position on these difficult issues is likely to fail. Rather, such differences should be celebrated as unique parts of His body, each with its own purpose and function. There is no such thing as a parachurch organisation as it cannot exist outside of the Church – rather they are essential specialist ministries. Claiming to be aligned with one person or denomination is, in Paul's words, carnal. God's Biblical nation consisted of twelve very different tribes and such tribal identities exist within and across the Church today – they are the glue that hold it together. The end-time destiny of the Church is probably a return to a thriving yet disparate underground entity pretty much as it was in the first three centuries. Only then will it have learned to speak with one voice and say "Come Lord Jesus".

I assume that you didn't find anything too contentious. Perhaps a question mark over one phrase, maybe. But consider this, if you are pretty much in agreement with this abstract then **why is His church so fragmented?** Do we have a shared blindness to the behaviours that may be hindering true demonstrable unity from happening?

Perhaps we need to dig a little deeper into the core ideas that we have developed throughout this book, which I can now summarise as follows:

1. There is only One Church, regardless of the diversity of congregations and denominations we may observe around us. This is fact and we should verbalise it as such at every opportunity.

2. We are commanded to love all people, and this includes all other Christians. Such love cannot merely be theoretical but must be seen by our actions regardless of whether we agree with those people or not. By this shall all men know that we are His disciples.

3. If someone claims to be a Christian, it is entirely up to God to decide whether they are genuine or not. The Holy Spirit inside us may alert us as to whether they are, but it is not our privilege to condemn them.

4. If we need a written statement of core Christian beliefs we can safely use the Nicene Creed as such a benchmark.

5. Beyond those core doctrines we are commanded to not condemn other Christians but to lovingly accept them all, even those who hold opposing doctrinal views. Such love is the backbone of our faith and without it the Church will fail in its mission to a fallen world.

6. The idea that one denomination is the only true one (i.e. a remnant) has no basis in scripture.

7. When it comes to the difficult issues that seek to divide us we don't need to change our convictions, but we shouldn't assume that our position is the 'Right One,' just that it is the 'Right One for Us.'

8. We must not use our position on any subject as the premise with which to condemn others because of their beliefs or practice. We do not have that right.

9. Attempts to find common doctrinal ground between opposing interpretations are destined to result in either something so vague it is meaningless or completely unacceptable to one party or the other.

10. If there are differences between us these are to be celebrated as we are all different and unique parts of His body, each with its own purpose and function. After all, without different notes you can't have harmony.

11. We must pro-actively choose to meet with those with different viewpoints, thus actively demonstrating love one for another.

12. Focussing on the differences between us will distract us, both personally and corporately from fulfilling our unique calling.

13. We must all find the place where we belong as without our part the body is lacking. But don't forget that we need all of the other parts too.

14. We must find our tribe – the group of like-minded people who share our God-given passions. These tribes exist both within and across congregations and are the glue that hold the entire body together.

15. Claiming to belong to one apostolic person (and by extension their apostolic stream or denomination) is, in Paul's words, carnal.

16. So-called parachurch organisations cannot exist outside of the One Church. These are Specialist Ministries and potentially may be a representation of the five-fold ministries of Ephesians 4v11.

17. As end-time persecution increases, the Church will probably thrive as an underground movement, not dissimilar to how it was in the first three centuries.

18. We should therefore not resist anything that helps the church become smaller and more disparate and yet stronger and more united.

19. It is exclusively God who builds His Church. He may choose to raise up cross-denominational leaders, or Deliverers, to lead the counterattack for His Church.

20. His end-time Church will ultimately speak with one voice to say "Come Lord Jesus." Perhaps we are delaying Christ's return by failing to act as one.

I am not saying that I am one hundred percent correct in all of these but having spent the last years immersed in Church history I have come away with a significant shift in my opinions. My responsibility was to document these alongside the book Ancient & Modern: The Search. It is up to you to decide if you share any of these ideas.

Thank you for reading.